Also available at all good book stores

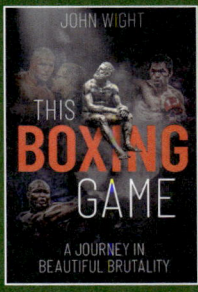

9781785316272

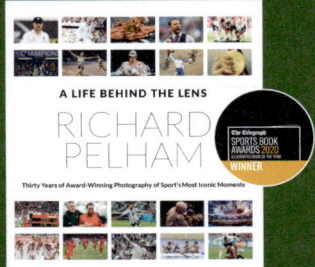

9781785315466

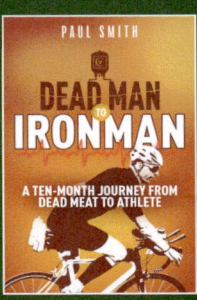

9781785316173

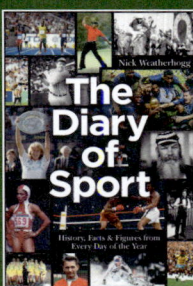

9781785316289

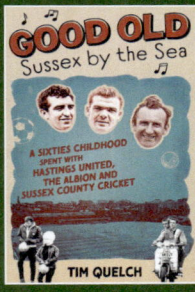

9781785316197

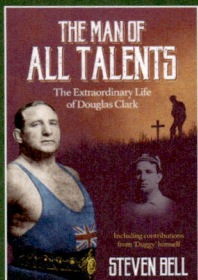

9781785316821

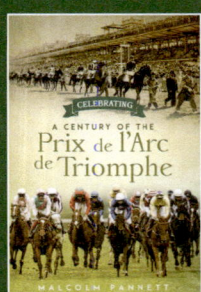

9781785317248

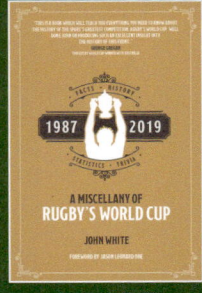

9781785315619

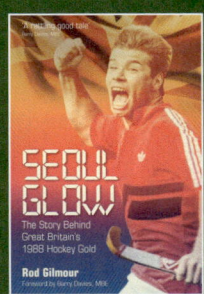

9781785314315

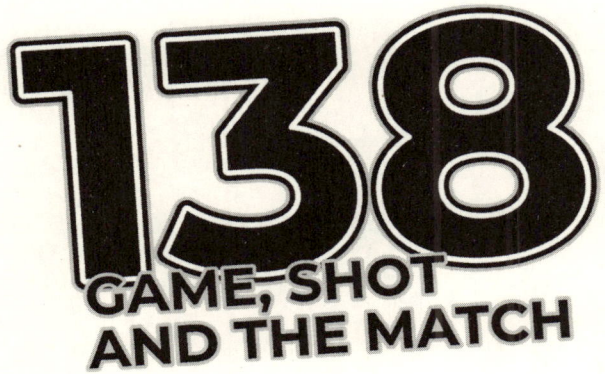

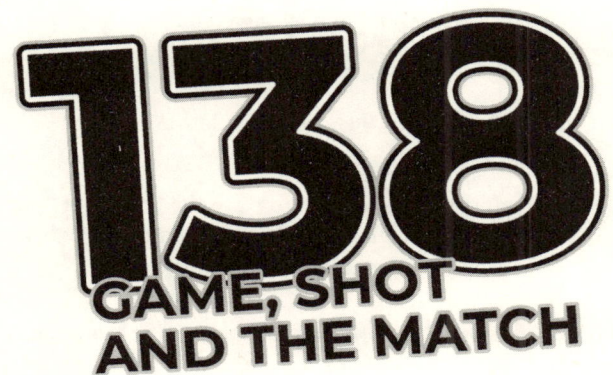

138
GAME, SHOT
AND THE MATCH

KEITH
DELLER

WITH EDWARD COUZENS-LAKE

First published by Pitch Publishing, 2021

Pitch Publishing
A2 Yeoman Gate
Yeoman Way
Worthing
Sussex
BN13 3QZ
www.pitchpublishing.co.uk
info@pitchpublishing.co.uk

A CIP catalogue record is available for this book
from the British Library.

ISBN 978 1 78531 787 3

Typesetting and origination by Pitch Publishing
Printed and bound in Great Britain by TJ Books, Padstow

Contents

To my wife, Kim, who has been
my soulmate and best friend for 36
years of my career, plus Lauren, my
daughter, and my son Matt, who have
both always supported their dad.

Foreword

IT'S IMPOSSIBLE to be a darts fan without being aware of the delightful presence of Keith Deller over the decades of the game's dazzling and spectacular growth.

It was his magical checkout of 138 in the 1983 World Championship Final that truly lit the darts spark in me, and in millions of others too. How this absurdly young prodigy, a qualifier for heaven's sake, could have beaten not just the all-conquering Eric Bristow, but the great John Lowe and the immortal Jocky Wilson on his way to the title, remains the stuff of legend.

But to those of us lucky enough to have seen something of how the modern game is broadcast we know that Keith is still at the very centre of the beating heart of darts. I have seen his skill and speed as a spotter close up and to me it was like watching a classical concert virtuoso.

A more liked and respected figure it would be hard to find in any sport. And now we are lucky enough to be able to read more about his life and story.

Turn the pages and enjoy.

Stephen Fry

Introduction

I HAVE KNOWN Keith ('Dynamite') Deller for my entire professional career and I can honestly say that he is without doubt the hardest-working player I have come across, a man who I would call a true professional.

Keith's belief in himself during the 1983 World Championship shows his true character – a mild-mannered man away from the oche but a fierce competitor on it.

Keith was also the first person to average over 100 in a televised game, an achievement that showed he had real quality.

He is a family man with a loving wife and two children. I am happy to call Keith Deller my friend.

Phil Taylor

Co-Author's Notes

IT'S ALWAYS a great conversation starter.

People ask me what I do for a living.

I tell them I'm a ghost.

You can probably work out for yourselves what comments inevitably follow.

The truth is, if you're a bit of a nosey so-and-so (the polite way of expressing it is to claim you are a 'people person') then ghost-writing is as good as it gets as a profession. I've ghosted quite a few biographies now. And can say, without exception, that I have enjoyed working on every single one of them. But working alongside Keith on this book has been a particular delight.

Those of you who already know him will nod your head in recognition of the fact when I say that Keith is a complete and utter gentleman.

The advent of Covid-19 in early 2020 and the immediate and long-lasting changes it has brought to all of our lives was a considerable challenge to us both when it came to writing this book, as the very core of writing any biography is the time that writer and subject spend together. Normally there are lots of face-to-face meetings held over numerous coffees in even more numerous bars, cafes and restaurants.

As it turned out, that was something we weren't going to be able to do any time soon.

So the fact that, despite this rather considerable obstacle threatening to derail the whole process right at the start, we've still managed to get the job done is something I am very proud of. But it would never have happened had it not been for Keith's commitment to the project, the diligence he has shown throughout and the massive amount of work he has put into every aspect of the book.

Like I said, he is a true gentleman. He'd ring me at around 5pm and, even before passing on the vital little snippet I'd asked for, or shared yet another recollection with me, he'd apologise for phoning me at what he considered to be an 'unsocial' hour. At the end of every discussion we had about the book, usually those relating to how we were going to push things forward and how I'd be working on doing that, he'd always say something along the lines of 'Is that all right with you, Ed?'

I suspect it's just one example of the polite consideration and courtesy he will show to anyone who he deals with in his day-to-day life. Keith's story is a remarkable one, to quote the words of Sid Waddell, the rise and rise of the 'kid from Suffolk' from playing in his kitchen to winning the World Darts Championship and everything that followed.

Keith shares his story with us in the easy-going, relaxed and occasionally self-effacing manner that his fans around the world have come to expect from him. It's a revealing and often funny one that contains more than its fair share of shocks and surprises, and is an honest and genuine exploration of a life well led told by a man who played a very big role in taking the game of darts to the wider audience it has always thoroughly deserved.

Edward Couzens-Lake

August 2021

Prologue

Quite what they felt about being constantly beaten
by one of the bar staff I don't know.

'I HEAR you are the top qualifier of the four here?'

The opening remarks of Peter Purves: actor, dog lover, former presenter of *Blue Peter* and now, among other things, the BBC's front man for their televised darts coverage. Which was, in this case, the 1983 BDO World Championship which was, back then, held at the Jollees Cabaret Club in Stoke-on-Trent.

He'd done his research at least. I was one of the four entrants in the final 32-man field who'd had to win the right to take part in the tournament by pre-qualifying, the same as Dave Lee, Peter Locke and Tony Ridler who'd won their place in the finals in the same way. There would have been some critics, of course, who would have commented that we were only there to make up the numbers and that our reward was simply being there and taking our place alongside the great and good of the game at the time. We were regarded, I suppose, in much the same way as a non-league football club is when it battles its way through to the FA Cup third round for their day in the sun. But that was as far as it went.

I had other ideas and I let Peter know that by looking him straight in the eye and saying, 'Yes, but I'm better than that, and I will be world champion by the end of the week.'

Fighting talk. And maybe that's how most would have seen it. A bit of bravado from the plucky qualifier, that sort of thing. You'd expect nothing else. But, unknown to me at the time, my words clearly made an impression on Peter because he promptly went out and put £20 on me to win the tournament at 66/1. Those were high odds that no bookie would ever expect to pay out on as, quite honestly, if you are the man, woman, team or horse who has those odds next to your name, then no one expects you to win.

But there were now two people at Jollees who thought I had a chance of going the whole way: myself and Peter Purves.

I'd been drawn to play Nicky Virachkul in the first round. He was the number seven seed for the tournament and had, in the previous two World Championships, got as far as the quarter-finals, losing to Eric Bristow in 1981 and Bobby George 12 months later. He'd also reached the World Masters semi-finals in 1980, beating, among others, Dave Whitcombe on the way, no mean feat as Dave is a great player who had, in 1982, won that tournament himself. So, make absolutely no mistake about it, I respected Nicky as both an opponent and fellow competitor.

But I knew I was going to beat him. Because Nicky and I had previous.

A year earlier, I'd been earning my living pulling pints at The Rising Sun pub at Whetstone in north London, where, shortly before the 1982 World Championship had commenced, Nicky, along with a few other overseas players, had popped in to have a couple of drinks as well as put in a little bit of practice. I quite fancied my chances against them as did, clearly, the landlord at the time, a chap by the name of Keith Cowan, who told me that as long as I stayed on the board and kept beating Nicky and his mates, I wouldn't have to take my usual place behind the bar.

I ended up spending three hours at board as neither Nicky nor any of the others could beat me. Quite what they felt about being constantly beaten by one of the bar staff I don't know but, at least as far as Nicky was concerned, it didn't affect his game too much as he went on to make the tournament's quarter-finals, beating Canadian Ray Kippari and Cliff Lazarenko en route before going out to Bobby George.

As far as I was concerned, I'd done more than enough to prove I could live with, match wise, some of the best darts players around. I hadn't had a lucky one-off win over one game of 501 or anything like that, I'd constantly beaten them, one after the other. So, even if they had been going a little bit easy on me to begin with (which I doubt) they'd soon have upped both their game and concentration after they'd lost a few games. That suited me. The ultimate way of testing yourself at any sport is to play against the best there is and I was making the most of my opportunity that afternoon, one that gave me very genuine hope that I'd be lining up alongside Nicky as one of the entrants in the World Championship at the start of the following year rather than pulling pints and collecting glasses for a living.

Twelve months of very hard work had followed and now, here I was, doing just that. A competitor at the 1983 World Darts Championship, taking my place alongside some of the greatest names to have ever played the game. The likes of Bobby George, Cliff Lazarenko, John Lowe, Leighton Rees and, of course, the Crafty Cockney himself, two-time winner and odds-on favourite for that year's tournament, the number one seed Eric Bristow.

Did I have enough self-belief to think that I could, if it came to it, beat Eric?

After all, beating Nicky was one thing. But Eric was on another level to the rest of us and well on his way to becoming one of the greatest players the game of darts has ever seen. He was, as the top seed, placed right at the top of the draw which meant that if we were to play against one another at all that week, it could only happen if we both made the final.

I was looking forward to it already.

Keith Deller

1

The Family Way

I can't imagine any of the current England players
mucking in with the kids on his local park!

IT WAS anything but a quiet family Christmas for the Dellers in 1959. And that's entirely my fault because, just as most people would, finally, have been starting to unwind come Christmas Eve and looked forward to the festivities ahead, I was keeping Mum fully occupied by making my big entrance into the world, minus, on that occasion, any sort of walk-on music, as their very own Christmas baby.

There were four of us in total. My dad, Derek Deller, was one of those blokes who pretty much kept himself to himself, a quiet man who thought nothing of walking three miles to and from work every day. He was an engineer who, for most of his life, worked for two big companies in Ipswich, one of which was called Ransomes, a manufacturer of agricultural machinery as well as a producer of general engineering products. Ransomes has always been an important part of Ipswich and is, I'm happy to say, still around to this day. He also worked for a different big local company called Cranes, another engineering company. He worked at nights while he was there so I didn't used to see him very much at all then as I'd be at school while he was getting some much-needed sleep at home then as, by 7pm, he'd be off to work. So we ended up like two ships passing in the night really for a while, my dad and I!

We soon got used to his unusual routine though because that meant he was in work and able to provide for the family, something which was always very important to the Deller family. Dad was a believer in working hard and looking after your family; simple but hugely important values. He'd do whatever it took in order to provide and to keep himself active. His last job was with Suffolk County Council and it was, you might say, a fairly humble one as he was a street cleaner. But he put as much energy and commitment into that job as he did everything else he did and, believe me, his 'beat' was always clean. He enjoyed it as well, saying on more than one occasion that it kept him fit and that he loved walking anyway, so it was the perfect job for him. He led by example and we lived a quiet and simple life, determined, at all times, never to let the family name down. Dad might have been a fairly unassuming chap but he was hugely proud of his family which was, by far, the most important part of his life.

Dad and I had a very good relationship. It was one that was very much based on respect. He was the breadwinner for the family which meant that he'd earned and deserved that from all of us. He used to remind me, all the time, to treat people with respect as well, and to always, for example, remember to say 'please' and 'thank you'. If I forgot to do so then, quite simply, I'd do without and, for all the fuss I might have made if this was the case, Dad and Mum would respond by looking me in the eye and saying, 'Keith, it costs nothing to say please or thank you.' They were right, of course, and I've never forgotten that.

We'd get a holiday every year. The destination never changed; it was always the holiday centre at Caister, which is near Great Yarmouth. Not that I minded, I loved it there and would throw myself into all the activities on offer. The excitement began, for me, with the drive there. Dad had an Austin Cambridge which he absolutely loved. It took about an hour to get to Caister in it from our house and I'd get more and more excited as we got ever closer. We'd go for a week and have the time of our lives although, funnily enough, I always used to dread the last night of that week as it meant saying goodbye to a whole load of new friends I'd made who I knew I'd never see again.

* * *

We lived on a council estate. People immediately think that it must have been a bit rough there but it wasn't at all, the people were friendly and there was a large green where all the children could play. By the time I was seven, I was very keen on playing football and would always be up there having a kick-around with my mates. I couldn't, mind you, head up there until I'd done my homework but, as soon as that was completed, on would go my football kit and I'd be off. We'd also congregate for a game in a park that was a bit further away at the bottom of the road. We'd play football there as well and, on occasion, would be joined by Kevin Beattie, the famous Ipswich Town and England centre-half who'd happily have a kick-around with us. I can't imagine any of the current England players mucking in with the kids on their local park.

I also enjoyed going to the pictures on a Saturday morning. That was always a treat and, in our day, it was one of the events of the week that you really looked forward to. Then, on Saturday evenings, we'd all go to visit Nanna and Grandad, Dad's parents, before heading off to a pub called the Margaret Catchpole. No prizes for guessing what Alan, my older brother, and I got up to there. Yes, we'd end up playing football with the children of all the other parents who were there. It meant a bit of peace and quiet for all the grown-ups I suppose, with all of us outside chasing a ball around while they had a drink and a natter. Mum would make sure we had a bottle of Coca-Cola and a packet of salt and vinegar crisps each, so we were happy. Saturdays were great as we always ended up going to bed late, which suited me.

I had the usual bumps and bruises as I was growing up, but nothing serious. I did, however, have a squint or, as it's referred to now, a lazy eye. I had an operation when I was five and it was successful, although the recovery time was long and, as a result of that, I had to give up my piano lessons as it made reading the music difficult for me at the time. Yes, in among all that childhood mucking about and playing football, there'd been time for me to get a bit of culture and learn the piano as well. I started having lessons when I was three, I only had to go to the next road to us for them, which was Woodpecker Road in Ipswich. I could read music by the time I was five and, who knows, maybe a different career beckoned? But then I had the operation and that was that, although it didn't, of course, ever prevent me from playing football. My eyesight improved as I got older and, over time, my left eye 'learned' to work harder to compensate for the fact my right eye was never going to be as good as it could be, even though my vision was fine. It's not really noticeable now unless you know, and Bobby George certainly does. He once said that looking at me was like a football match, 'one [eye] at home and one away'.

Dad particularly enjoyed his Saturdays as there would always be horse racing on TV in the afternoons, including, if you remember, the ITV Seven on *World of Sport*, the programme that was introduced by Dickie Davies. Dad would be up (despite not having to go to work) at 7am every Saturday to get his paper from the local shop so he could spend a happy three hours or so checking the form before spending the afternoon sat in front of the television. Dad loved his telly; his favourite programmes were *Laurel and Hardy* and *Dad's Army*. I found both of them funny as well and would often sit with him and watch them when they were on. Mind you, he nearly ended up appearing on TV himself once when he popped outside only to find there were TV cameras all over the place. The BBC were using a back street in the centre of Ipswich to film part of an *Only Fools and Horses* episode, the one where Rodney is employed by an undertaker as the chief mourner and ends up taking the hearse up a one-way street. The makers must have thought that road in Ipswich looked a little like Peckham in London as they used the junction of Seymour Road and Rectory Road for filming.

Dad wasn't always stuck inside though, and he liked to play a spot of sport at times. His was bowls and he'd regularly play at the Margaret Catchpole bowls club with his brother Roy.

* * *

Christmas was always a happy time. Dad and Mum might not have had much to spend but they made it special every year. It was an especially exciting time for me of course, as my birthday is on Christmas Eve, so I got presents two days running. That sounds great until you realise, of course, that's it for the rest of the year. On one particular birthday, I'd had such a good time that I couldn't get to sleep, no matter how much I tried. It was the same for Alan so, when Dad, dressed up as Father Christmas, came into our bedroom later that evening with all of our presents, we knew it was him and both said, 'Hello Dad.' I think that he was actually quite happy to hear us say that, as it meant he'd never have to put that big old red and white suit on again!

Dad may have been glad he didn't have to wear the Father Christmas outfit again, but one item of clothing I was always ready to wear and at any time of the year was a football shirt.

My life revolved around playing football or talking about playing football, or watching football. I loved all the different kits and, although Ipswich Town were very definitely my team, I also liked West Ham and loved their claret and blue strip. But it was always Ipswich for me. We had a great time through the 1970s and 80s. Bobby Robson, who was the team's manager, knew a good player when he saw one and we had plenty. Mick Mills was as good a defender as anyone, and he played in the 1982 World Cup finals for England as did Terry Butcher and Paul Mariner, who sadly passed away while this book was being written.

We also had the two Dutch midfield maestros, Arnold Mühren and Frans Thijssen, who came over to play in England when having a continental player in your team was still a rarity. Both were quality and I loved watching them play. Town would often feature on *Match of the Week*, which was Anglia TV's weekly football programme. Watching that show was a bit of a ritual for us all on Sunday afternoons and we'd make sure we finished our dinner in time so we were all cleared up and ready when it came on. Mum would spend all of Sunday mornings making a lovely roast dinner for us all and, being a lad who liked his food, and with the football to come, it became one of my favourite days of the week. That is, I should add, unless there was kippers for tea. I absolutely hated them but not half as much as I hated liver and bacon which she'd make sure we had at least once a week. On those days I'd either have beans on toast or go out for fish and chips. I must have eaten a lot of beans on toast mind, as I'd also have them on Shrove Tuesday because, guess what, I don't like pancakes either. As for liver and bacon, don't even get me started on that (because I won't and would rather go hungry). Fish and chips does me fine, it always has done, so whenever Mum and Dad were having something for tea I didn't see eye to eye with, it was off to the chippy for me.

Like all youngsters at the time, I looked forward to the ice cream man coming round in his van. Mr Softy would regularly oblige and Mum and Dad would always make sure that we got an ice cream from him. On one occasion, however, I was so excited to hear his van's distinctive chimes outside that I kicked my football through the living room window. I knew straight away that my chances of getting an ice cream after doing that were not particularly good, and I was right. I did get a smacked bottom and was told I was grounded.

If I wasn't playing or watching football, then it's fairly safe to say that Alan and I would be laying on the floor playing the Subbuteo football game. We took it very seriously and even had the floodlights, which weren't cheap to buy at all. I'd enjoy playing that but only if I was winning as I was, as Alan found to his cost, a very bad loser, so much so that, if he beat me at a game, I'd break a few of his players in retaliation.

* * *

When I was eight years old, I remember Dad saying he wasn't feeling very well, which was unusual for him. He told us that he had bad indigestion but, seconds after he said that, he started to behave very strangely, so much so, that Mum called an ambulance. He was then very sick. I was holding a bowl for him to be sick into but could see that he was bringing up a lot of blood, which was very scary. I actually think we were close to losing him at one point and all I wanted to hear was the sound of the ambulance's siren as it pulled up outside our house. I had to be strong for Mum but also for Alan, who was so upset that he got into a terrible state. Mind you, I felt pretty helpless myself but tried my best to comfort Dad. He got to the hospital just in time where a duodenal ulcer was diagnosed.

That was all a bit touch and go as he'd lost a lot of blood. It remains, as you won't be surprised to read, one of the darkest and most upsetting memories of what was otherwise a very happy and contented childhood.

Mum, on the other hand, was a more outward kind of person, the sort who would do anything for anybody. She was a proper Suffolk girl and had met Dad during the war. She originally worked at the local butcher's shop along with her sister Irene on the Chantry Estate. She progressed from there to the local Sainsbury's where she ended up working for many years until she retired – and she didn't want to do that, she would have preferred to carry on working! She also had a little job that she used to do from home, called Shopacheck; people in and around the local neighbourhood would buy things from her and she'd do a weekly round where she collected their money. It was a team effort really as Dad would drive her to all the places that she needed to go to, which was a good idea, especially on the dark and cold winter nights as she'd quite often have a lot of money on her.

Dad wasn't from Suffolk. He was a 'furriner' as they say in East Anglia, a Londoner who was brought up in Fulham. He had a cousin who we called Uncle Mol, who lived above a bank at Seven Sisters tube station. If we happened to be there when Tottenham were playing at home, I used to look out of the window watching all the football fans and police horses coming and going, which was exciting for any young child just as the train ride down to London always was for me. Mum and Dad would also take us out on Sundays. We'd usually head down to Walton-on-the-Naze, which is a small town on the Essex coast.

We'd meet up with assorted uncles, aunties and cousins and have a big family day out, one that usually involved a lot of football (which suited me just fine) and cricket as well as copious amounts of fish and chips from one of the shops on the seafront which, surprise surprise, suited me down to the ground as well. I knew and got on with everyone in my extended family. The only members I never knew were Mum's parents as, despite their never having smoked or drank in their lives, they both died when they were just 49. I also had an uncle who I never knew, one of Dad's brothers, who was run over by an army tank.

They were proper family days out, real happy times.

It wasn't all fun and games as I was growing up mind you. I don't want you thinking that life for the young Keith Deller was nothing but a rich mix of football, television and days at the seaside. No, there was also my education to take into consideration.

My first school was Gusford Primary which is on the Chantry Estate, a familiar sight and, I am sure, memory, for all the hundreds of kids who were born there. It was a fairly small school, so you never felt as if you were going to be overwhelmed there as you might at a bigger one, plus, and this was an advantage as far as I was concerned, it was only a ten-minute walk from our house. This was especially good in the mornings as it was all downhill but, by the end of the school day when I'd be tired and wanting to get back, repeating that same walk again uphill was something that I hated. Mind you, there was usually something to do in the evenings so I wouldn't be tired for very long. That included joining the Cub Scouts, which I did was I was seven, then, once I'd left Gusford, I joined a youth club that was part of the setup at my new school.

The natural route to take after you left Gusford was to go to the 'big school' from the age of 11 which, for me, was Chantry High School. It was comprised of four big buildings that were all marked out in different colours. Being an Ipswich Town fan, I was pleased to be allocated to 'Blue' building. I was never going to be a budding academic, though, and the only thing I tried really hard to do every day was to get a window seat in the classroom so I could while away whatever lesson I was in gazing out of it and on to whatever was happening in the world outside.

* * *

That's not to say I didn't work hard. I did reasonably well at all of my lessons and was never really in trouble or anything, it was just that my main focus was on sport. I had trials for Suffolk at basketball while I was at Chantry High as well as going on to represent my home county at table tennis, something that made me very proud. Yet, despite all that, the real love of both my school and sporting life was always football.

One of my mates at Chantry House was a boy called Terry Westley. We both played up front for the school football team and weren't a bad little combination. Terry went on to have a very decent career as a football coach and has had spells as manager of both Derby County and Luton Town. He was, until 2019, the academy manager at West Ham where, among others, he was responsible for coaching Declan Rice, who is now a full England international.

I bet he never thought he'd get that far in the game when we were getting kicked all over the place by opposition defences when we were both playing for Chantry High.

While I was at school, I was lucky enough to be selected as one of the ball boys for matches at Portman Road, home of, as if you didn't know, the one and only Ipswich Town. It was quite an involved job in those days mind you, as, apart from the obvious duties connected with the role, we also had to put the half-time scores up on a big board as there were no electronic scoreboards back then.

It was great fun though, especially as it meant you had access to, and saw things, that the average fan never came close to seeing. We'd be based directly opposite the away team's dressing rooms for example, as that was where the club's boot room was. On one Saturday when Manchester United were playing Ipswich, one of their members of staff popped his head around our door and asked me to clean one of their players' boots – the late and very great George Best. I did the job and I must have ended up putting too much polish on them as, thankfully, he didn't score against us in that match.

On another occasion the great Leeds United team of Don Revie were in town. They used to have little tags that they tucked into their socks which had the players' shirt numbers on them. This was quite a revolutionary thing at the time as no other team did it, or, I think, has ever done it since. I was lucky enough to get hold of the tags that had been worn during the match by Mick Jones, who was their centre-forward, so they both had '9' printed on them. I couldn't wait to get home that afternoon and show them to my parents.

Mind you, it wasn't all fun and games being a ball boy at Ipswich. The hardest part of the job was if you ended up being situated in front of the away fans. They'd usually take delight in doing things like filling little paper bags with dirt or whatever they could get their hands on and throw them at me. That said, as we had such a great team in those days, we usually beat whoever we were playing, so I tended to have the last laugh most of the time.

As far as I am concerned, the greatest player to have ever worn the Ipswich Town shirt is the late Kevin Beattie, who, if you remember, would occasionally join all of us kids for a kick-about in the park at the bottom of my road. Kevin lived in a house that was owned by the club and only a couple of minutes or so walk from my home. He'd sometimes see me at the bus stop opposite our house waiting for the bus that would take me to Portman Road and stop so he could give me a lift there, which made all of my friends very envious of me. Kevin and I eventually became good friends and I used to love watching him play. He was a genuine natural and a player who always looked so comfortable on the ball. Unfortunately for him and for football, his career was cut short by injuries and he started to find the going very tough indeed. I tried to help him in any way that I could and when, for example, I heard he was going to have to sell his FA Cup winner's medal in 1983 (I was at Wembley on that great day in 1978 when we beat Arsenal in the final), I knew I couldn't bear the thought of Kevin's medal going to a complete stranger so I bought it from him, took it home and kept it safe in a drawer. A year or so later, when Kevin was getting on a lot better than he had been, he happened to ask me about his medal and if I had sold it. I said there was no way I would ever have sold it and gave it back to him, saying I didn't want anything for it as we were good friends.

Watching Ipswich play as a youngster remains one of the great memories of my life and a very happy one. We had a magnificent team throughout the 1970s and 80s, winning, during that time, the FA Cup as well as the UEFA Cup, one of only five English teams to have won that particular trophy. We've taken on and beaten some great teams in European competition over the years including FC Cologne, Feyenoord,

Lazio, Real Madrid and Roma as well as running Barcelona mighty close on a couple of occasions.

Alan was a couple of years or so older than me and, as a consequence of that, he took on the responsibilities of having a younger sibling very seriously and would worry himself silly if, for whatever reason, I didn't come home on time. I rather think that shows him up as a typical 'people person', someone who cares as much for the welfare of other people as he does himself. He would have got that from Mum, who was always there if needed, and was ever ready to answer a call to arms if someone in the family or the Chantry Estate was in need of something or were just a bit down on their luck. Alan ultimately took his people skills into a professional setting and was, for a very long time, one of the porters at Ipswich's hospital.

Not long after I'd left school, Alan got me a job at the Tooks Bakery, which was on the Old Norwich Road in Ipswich. My job there was a very tedious one indeed as all I did all day was make the boxes that the cakes went in. For hour after hour after hour.

Still, at least it meant I was earning a little bit of money. I was lucky enough to have a cousin who also worked at Tooks and was one of the supervisors, so, after around six months or so of making boxes, I got promoted and was now entrusted to work on the ovens. I was responsible for stacking all the trays with the pre-baked goods, from sausage rolls to pies, up on to the racks in the ovens so they could be cooked. I soon had a way of getting this done really quickly but, if my cousin happened to be around, we'd end up chatting about sport as I was working, so it wasn't unknown for anyone who might have been working in the ovens at the time to hear a loud crash as I dropped the occasional tray. I'd then have to stop the belt, get rid of all the mess and carry on as before, taking care not to do it again as I didn't want to run the risk of losing my job, boring as it was.

Christmas at Tooks saw the annual staff party, something that everyone would start talking about weeks before it actually took place – well, you couldn't be spending all of your time debating the finer merits of our sausage rolls. The company would book five coaches and they'd all be packed out as we descended from Ipswich to Felixstowe. It was always a good night out but, unfortunately, it also had the tendency to end with a massive punch-up as the mix of too much alcohol and the various relationships between different men and women started to provoke the usual aggression between people from the different estates in Ipswich. I never got involved in any of the fighting and always kept well out of it but, as time went by, I realised that neither the work nor the social life that Tooks had to offer was for me, and quit. I did have some fond memories of the place mind you and, after I'd won the World Championship in 1983 I called in to say hello to some of the people I knew still worked there, but didn't, sadly, get the welcome I thought I might. It felt as if that was down to plain old jealousy and envy at what I had achieved since I'd left, which was a shame as it had never been my intention to go there and do the old 'look at me now' thing – I just wanted to catch up with a few old mates.

One of my best friends also happened to be one of Alan's friends, David Goldrick, or 'Sos' as he was known to his mates. We'd all meet up on Friday and Saturday nights at a pub called The Kingfisher, regular as clockwork and always at 7pm. We'd stay there for a couple of hours or so before heading out on a pub crawl around some of the other good pubs in Ipswich and ending the night at the Tracey's nightclub where we'd all attempt to go 'on the pull'. I'd always put in a bit of extra effort on those nights, so out would come my best jacket which was a rather nice, if I say it myself, checked number so, what with that and my Brut aftershave, I saw myself as quite the potential catch – in my dreams at least. At the end of the evening and, of course, after we had all invariably failed to 'pull', we'd end up at the local Chinese restaurant for a meal and more laughs.

One nightclub I used to go to was called the First Floor Club, which was owned by a chap called Ken Beam. It was popular among the Ipswich Town footballers so, naturally enough, that meant it was somewhere I wanted to go to as well. Not long after I'd won the World Championship, I went there for a relaxing night out but it turned out to be anything but that, as Ken would announce over the club's PA, 'We have Keith Deller in the club tonight,' and he'd promptly put a replay of my final against Eric on all the screens which was a bit embarrassing for me.

But it was a great place to go to when I was younger and no one knew who I was. I couldn't be too hung over though as I played football for two different teams on Sundays, as well as for one on Saturdays. Of those games and the leagues we played in, the Sunday morning match was, by far, the toughest one. All 22 players would, invariably, still be in a bit of a state from the previous night's exertions so there were always a few late and dodgy tackles flying in and you rarely saw out 90 minutes without at least one player getting sent off. I still enjoyed it though and only packed in playing as I was getting more into my darts so couldn't afford to have any sort of bad injury, especially, of course, to my arms or hands.

'Getting more into my darts'?

I blame Mum and Dad for everything. When I was about 13, they set up a dartboard in the house, just as thousands of parents must have done for their children over the years, hundreds and hundreds of thousands probably.

It was something for them to do when they couldn't go out, so it would keep them occupied. Plus, of course, it was something we could all join in with as well; another fun family activity for a wet weekend. It was good practice for them anyway, as they both played in league teams whose matches were played at The Kingfisher. So I started throwing darts around in our kitchen with them.

When I picked up a dart for the first time, it felt good to give the game a go, as well as watch Mum and Dad playing in the kitchen – and playing it very well from what I could see. I loved hitting the trebles and it felt great every time I did so, which meant I was getting more and more of a buzz for the game every time I picked the darts up and my enthusiasm and interest was growing. I soon started to hit the treble 20s regularly, which is something that the very great majority of players simply cannot do. I then knew that not only was I improving at this game but did seem to be rather good at it.

So, quite unexpectedly, football suddenly had a rival for my sporting affections.

2

Lightning Never Strikes Twice

*It was a defeat that hit me hard and yes, it hurt
as well but there is a saying about how you need
to lose before you learn to win.*

SO, THERE was now a dartboard in our kitchen. Interesting.

Mum and Dad insisted, of course, that it was there so they could both practise for their league matches up at The Kingfisher. Which they did, regularly. What they might not have expected, however, was to have such a keen practice companion. I found that I enjoyed throwing the darts and, before long, I was more than capable of getting some high scores every time we played.

By the time I was 15, I was in the Kingfisher team myself although, looking back, we played on what is known as an Ipswich (or Kent) Five's dartboard. They're not numbered in the traditional sense like a standard dartboard, but, as the name suggests, in multiples of five. Twenty is still at 12 o'clock while, rather than three at six o'clock, there is a 15. Twenty different scoring opportunities as normal but with either a five, ten, 15 or 20 in them. Anyway, that's the board we played on and it was also the one we had at home, firmly fixed to the kitchen wall. If we had been playing for a long time or if the darts hit the wall a few times, our neighbour, Mrs Sparks would knock from her side of the dividing wall that Dad had fixed the board to.

I entered The Kingfisher's singles tournament in 1974 when I was just 15, thinking it would be a great experience as well as a bit of a learning curve, up against players who were better than me and learning a few lessons in the process. That meant I had to go on and represent the pub's team in games against all of the other teams in that league, a daunting prospect for someone as young as I was. But the whole of the rest of the team came along to support me on the night and yes, I did feel the pressure, no doubt about that. However, I went on to win the competition, which was a bit of a surprise for a few people I suppose, especially as some of the battle-hardened regulars might not have enjoyed seeing a 15-year-old schoolboy walk away with the trophy. But, as far as I was concerned, that was only the beginning. My journey into darts and all the success I've had was well and truly under way.

I was one of the youngest playing and, again, always thought a tournament would be a great experience for me, but I ended up, around eight times out of ten, winning them as well. Winning things, no matter what sport you are playing, is infectious – as soon as you've won something you end up wanting to play and win it again. That was exactly what I felt and, in time, I started, with all of that raw confidence that you have when you are young, to believe I was the best player in the area, something which was only reinforced when I won the super league singles title.

I clearly needed to step up yet another level. Just how far could I go? In 1976, when I was still only 17, Bob Rossiter, who, with his wife Pam owned a pub called The Albion Mills in Ipswich, took me under his wing. It had a very good reputation as the best pub to play darts at in Suffolk as they were really committed to both the game and players by holding a monthly tournament on Sundays. The competitors would be made up of 16 players in total, most of whom were either Suffolk County 'A' or 'B' team players. The matches would be split into two with eight playing in the main bar while the other eight played in the lounge bar, with the eventual winner from each bar playing in the final for a prize of £10.

For me, at just 17, this was the serious and regular practice that I now needed against good opposition. I won a lot of these events, but it was never easy and some of the people I came up against were very good players like, for example, Eddie Brown from Stoneham who'd won the News of the World Championship in 1962. But I kept making progress. When I was 18, Mum and I won the mixed pairs title at our pub, going on to do so for the following two years after that. I got a lot of pleasure out of winning that one for the simple reason that I was teamed up with her and it seemed more about having fun than being under any sort of pressure to win. It wasn't quite the same with Dad, who'd come and watch me play and, if I wasn't doing well, I'd look over to where he was sitting and he'd be shaking his head in disbelief at what was happening.

Bob Rossiter would very kindly pay my tournament entry fees for me as he knew just how valuable regular competition was. I was already, by then, playing in his Monday night darts team as well as in the Tuesday night super league matches for Bob. But he wanted me to play more and said I should now be considering playing in some of the open events against players who I didn't already know and, of course, because of that, didn't have any idea about what they were like or how they approached a game. Some of them were among the leading names in the sport at the time, top players such as Eric Bristow, Cliff Lazarenko and Bobby George. These events were sometimes played at venues that might have been as far as three hours or so away, but Bob would never accept my offers of petrol money and was, at the time, one of the people who gave me the most help and advice about getting on in the game. It's a friendship and generosity of spirit that I have never forgotten and will always be grateful for.

I'd also, at this time, been selected to play for Suffolk. We had a good county team, good enough to reach the national finals where we were drawn to play against Derbyshire. My match was against the then world number two John Lowe and I have to admit, as familiar as I was becoming at playing in tournaments and having matches against some very good players, the thought of playing against one of the true greats of the game made me very nervous and I ended up losing 3-0 to John. I've never liked losing and was in a bad mood as we made our way home on the coach, but Bob reassured me, saying it was all part of the learning curve.

That was the year that Eric Bristow came along to one of the local clubs to take on some of the best players in Suffolk. The format of these games was good for the professionals as it would be over one game only and from 1001 – so you'd need lots of constantly high three-dart scores from the start to have a chance of winning, which was the sort of consistency that a pro would be able to put together fairly easily but not so easy for the amateur, however good they were. Eric already knew that I was the best player in Suffolk and said I could come on last that night, except it would be five legs over 1001 rather than just the one. He wanted to put on a show in that last 'showpiece' match of the evening against me but was also confident that he'd win over the five legs. Except he didn't. I won and the 250 people there went mad. Eric's response was to get on the microphone and say:

'Lightning never strikes twice.'

So we played again, exactly the same format and exactly the same result: 3-2 to me. It was a great experience and a memory that I will always hold close to my heart but, more than that, the pressure of playing against him in such a long match would, one day, serve me well in what turned out to be the biggest game of my life.

I ended 1976 as the Suffolk County darts champion, so my sporting career was heading in the right direction.

It wasn't just darts at the time mind you, as I still loved my football back then – and that was playing the game as well as watching and supporting Ipswich Town. By 1978, when I was 18, I was playing for two different football teams, one of which competed in a Saturday morning league. I enjoyed playing in those matches, especially as the other team I played for had their matches on a Sunday morning. There is just one word to describe those games, the teams and most of the other players who played in them: brutal.

* * *

It was a league where the point of most of the games seemed to be far more about kicking the opposition players than the ball but, given they were played before midday, a lot of the players would turn up more than a little hung over from the previous night's fun and games, so most of them didn't really seem bothered about whether they played the ball or the man and, as a result, there were always, as I've already said, a few dismissals in most of the games I played in. Watching all of this go on around me helped me to realise that there was every chance of getting a serious injury in one of these matches if, for whatever reason, one of the opposing players took a disliking to me so I decided to hang up my boots and start to take my darts a lot more seriously.

As it turned out, that was a decision I made at just about the right time as, not long afterwards, a darts player who I used to play with at the Albion Mills on Monday nights, Pat Andrews, had taken me to one side and had a quiet word. He used to work out in Saudi Arabia on a one month on and one month off basis so, given that he loved darts and could afford both the time and money to do so, he offered to sponsor me for £60 a week over a year on the condition that, whenever he was at home, I would regularly practise with him. This was great for me as, because of Bob Rossiter's help in getting me to play in more and more tournaments, I needed all the practice I could get. Mind you, after a few sessions with Pat, I'm not sure my liver would have been quite so appreciative.

But things were now beginning to happen because, in that same year, Bobby George got in touch and said I should come and join him and a few others over the pond to take part in the North American Open where the four-man team I was in, along with Bobby, Dave Lee and Colin Baker, beat formidable opposition in Eric Bristow, John Lowe, Cliff Lazarenko and Leighton Rees in the final. It was a big stage, a big event and one that featured all of the biggest names in the sport so I guess, as I was, by far, the youngest and most inexperienced, certainly at that level, there, little was expected of me. Yet Bobby would not have asked me to join his team to make up the numbers or for any sentimental reasons like 'giving the young lad a go'. He'd have wanted to win as would Dave and Colin and I'd have been expected to play my part.

Put it another way, this was no holiday. I played really well throughout, not that it was difficult to do so what with being surrounded by older and more experienced players who you can talk to and learn from – and I did. I ended up hitting two 180s during the tournament and my only real weakness at the time was my counting. You do need to be a bit quick with the numbers and all the possible permutations when you play darts at the highest level. If, for example, you enjoy a game with your mates at the pub and you need 158 to win, you probably aren't even going to think about what you need to get that score in three darts, you're just going to go for a high score and leave yourself something easy to finish up on. You can't do that at the highest level. If you're at the oche with a score like that left and the referee is saying, 'Keith, you require 158,' then you've got to know, immediately, how you are going to throw that number.

That was how it turned out for me in the final. It was the best of three and we were 1-0 up, needing 158 for the match. The best way to get there is (I bet you've done it already?) treble 20, treble 20 and double 19. Except that, as I said to Bobby, 'Bobby, I don't like double 19 if I go treble 20 and treble 20.'

In an instant, Bobby answered, 'Just go treble 18, treble 18 and bull.'

He'd worked out that permutation a lot more quickly than I'd have been able to. But he wasn't finished yet.

'Make sure you hit it!'

I'm not sure if he was joking or not with that last bit. But he had a look in his eye that suggested that he expected me to do as he'd said so I threw that combination to check out and win the match, much to Bobby's amusement, as he couldn't stop laughing afterwards.

Our opponents didn't find it funny though. They were a very strong quartet and had been expected to win, so I think the last thing any of them expected was not only to lose, but for the match-winning throw to have been made by a teenager who had, in the process, stolen the thunder of the current (Rees) and soon to be (Lowe) world champions. I'd like to think that they and Eric made a note of my name on that day.

I was now starting to enter some of the bigger tournaments, which meant I'd be up against the likes of Eric, John and Leighton a lot more often, with one of the earliest possibilities of doing so coming in the Eastern Counties leg of the 1979 News of the World Championship in Ipswich. Winning it would, of course, have been great, but, more than that, the eventual champion would have qualified for the finals of what was then a very prestigious tournament as you made your way there by winning a series of regional events.

Eight players took part on the night, having reached that stage by coming through pub and then county level play-offs. The winner would go on to play in the national finals at the Alexandra Palace in London, an event that not only drew in a large (and raucous) paying audience of 10,000 people but would also be shown live on ITV. The hot favourite that year was Eric Bristow but, before I got the chance to play against Eric, I had to win that Eastern Counties leg where I ended up being drawn to play against Bobby George in the first round. He was the last person I wanted to come up against at that early stage but, for all that, I had a lot of the brash confidence about me that you get when you are young and feeling indestructible, so I focused on getting into my game zone, looked over at Bobby, and just thought, 'Bring it on.'

I played well in the first leg of our match but missed three darts at double 20, which is pretty unforgivable at any level, especially one as high as this. The format for the event was the best of three legs (and playing from 8ft, rather than the standard 7ft 9.25in) which meant if you lost the first leg, then the pressure was immediately on you to win the next, else you'd be gone and on the way home. So I was really disappointed to have missed my chances at winning that first leg against Bobby but managed to start the second leg well only, for a second time, to end up missing three darts at double top which meant, for me, the dream of winning that particular title was over for another year. Bobby went on to win the event, saying to me as we had a quick chat that I had to learn how to lose before I learned to win. It was great advice from a top player that I immediately took to heart and have never forgotten.

Bobby was unstoppable that night and didn't lose a single leg as he went on to win the trophy at the Ally Pally by beating Alan Glazier 2-0. I tell him to this day that I let him off on the night, to which he offers back a big smile and a photograph of him with the trophy. He was in great form at the time as he'd won the singles at the North American Open the previous year (1978), beating Len Heard in the final, as well as, in 1979, winning the Butlin's Grand Masters, where he beat Bill Lennard in the final, then defended the title in 1980 against Leighton Rees. He also in 1980 reached the final of the BDO World Championship, losing 5-3 to Eric. He was, in short, the type of player I would have to look to beat six, seven, maybe eight times out of ten if

I was ever going to have the same sort of profile and success in the game as he was at that time.

I must mention, as a quick aside, how easy it was to enter the News of the World Championship. The newspaper would include an application form within its sports pages for a few Sundays in the weeks leading up to the qualifiers, which meant, even if you'd never thrown a dart before in your life, you could still enter it and end up playing against one of the game's greats in the final stages – providing, of course, you got past the very early stages of the competition which were held in pubs and clubs all over the country. I'm sure there were a few people who filled out the form and entered the tournament, which was one of the more prestigious on the darts calendar, for a bit of a laugh, reckoning that, as they occasionally had a game with their mates on a Saturday night at the pub, they could give this one a go. They would have soon discovered just how high the standard of play was with a lot of the men who took the game a little more seriously and certainly wouldn't have made much progress in the tournament had they actually got as far as playing a game.

It was a significant year for me, 1979. For one thing, I started doing a lot of exhibition matches throughout all of Suffolk. Not for myself mind you, but for a young girl whose story had reached one of the local papers. She badly needed a dialysis machine and was struggling to raise the funds needed so, along with a friend of mine by the name of Enos Fenner, we arranged and played a series of exhibition matches over the next two years or so and managed, between us, to raise around £15,000 for her, something we were both really pleased we'd been able to do. There was another upside to the story however, as all that travelling around and playing lots of games in a wide variety of locations and against opponents of varying ability and character gave me a lot of experience of what it would be like to be on the exhibition circuit.

With such thoughts in mind, it seems fitting now that I met John Markovic around that time. John was from Serbia and played a massive role behind the scenes in darts, especially in the early 1990s when he had a very influential role in the formation of the World Darts Council, which is now known as the Professional Darts Corporation (PDC). Lots of good people were involved as well, including Tommy Cox, Dick Allix, Edward Lowy and Unicorn Darts as well as John Raby, who put on the events and did the stage set-ups as well as Marcus Robertson.

John and his partner, Linda Batten, also represented Bob Anderson and Steve Brennan so they knew darts and how it worked. They also, clearly, realised just how much potential it had to grow far away and beyond the game that people had, for so long, associated with smoky bars and clubs. So I was delighted to team up with their organisation, especially as Linda had been quoted as saying that their role as far as their clients was concerned, was to do 'everything barring throwing the darts'.[1] That arrangement suited me as it meant I knew I would be able to get on and improve my game without having to think

---

1   From 'Interview with Linda Duffy' for www.globaldarts.de

about anything else as, whatever that was, someone else would be dealing with it for me.

Linda was a very decent darts player indeed at that time. She was the number one in the women's game from 1982 through to 1987, having started playing in her local pub when she was 15. This was unusual for, at that time, women simply didn't play darts. It wasn't, I should add, that they were barred from playing or anything like that, but that there was simply little to no opportunity for them to do so at even the most basic of competitive levels as there was no such thing as county ladies darts until the mid-1970s. Darts was seen as a man's game but Linda changed all that and ended up playing for the England national team for a decade, and on many occasions as captain. She went on to win the ladies' singles competition in the women's WDF (World Darts Federation) Europe Cup in 1984 followed by, a year later, winning the ladies' singles at the WDF World Cup – so, all in all, not a bad couple, really, to entrust with looking out for you in darts.

I'd often stay at John and Linda's when I was playing in London, especially when I had super league fixtures to take part in at the Victoria pub in Tottenham. They were tough matches as I'd usually be up against England internationals but, again, it was all good experience for me in that I was now regularly playing against some of the best in the game but in a lively environment, something you have to be used to and able to cope with if you are ever going to play darts at a high level.

What do you need to be able to play at the very highest level though, the one I was now proving I was capable of consistently doing? It's a question I'm asked a lot and, for me, there are three answers. First and very foremost, you need to practise regularly. And by that, I mean for several hours and every day. And that's <u>every</u> day. It means that you get into a good rhythm with your throw and technique and are so 'in the zone' that you can go out there and hit the shots and scores that you need from the off. But that's not all.

You also have to possess self-belief in abundance. Darts is, and excuse me for stating the obvious, an individual game, so the onus is on you to deliver and if you don't or can't, it's no one else's fault but your own. Finally, you need to be able to deal with pressure. High pressure and expectations. And constantly. If you break out into a nervous sweat before you step up to play Phil Taylor, he is, quite simply, going to annihilate you. So you've not only got to cope with standing on a stage with him, together with a vigorous and likely partisan audience as well, but also all the paraphernalia of live television into the bargain. That's bright lights and cameras all over the place as well as the growing realisation that millions of people are going to be watching you in their homes. So you've got to love playing darts. If you don't think you will, then I'm sorry, but, as good a player as you might be, I don't think professional darts is going to be the game for you.

The great players, the Phil Taylors of this world, love pressure. They positively thrive on it in fact – and the more of it there is, the more they like it. I once had a chance to win the World Championship with three darts. Now that **was** pressure, especially as Eric Bristow was up there standing next to me, eager, ready and more than capable of stepping in if I couldn't cope with the pressure that was on me at that precise moment. But more about that later.

That was a long way off at the time though. I needed to keep practising, learning and playing. And regularly. So another thing that helped push me along in the right direction that year was that trip out to America to play some of the world's best. It took me right out of my comfort zone, it wasn't like playing in the comfortable and familiar surroundings of some of the pubs and clubs I knew in Suffolk. In the US, I had to be switched on and ready to play my best game from the off, there was no time to settle down or place to hide, and certainly no excuses. It's you, the oche and the dartboard and you have to perform well for all those people that have paid good money to see you.

I returned to America in 1981 to play in three tournaments but this time it would be as an individual rather than, as it had been two years earlier, as part of a team. I'd been asked to go by fellow competitor and England international Tony Sontag (who'd made a bit of a name for himself by winning the Swedish Open the previous year) with Tony waiting until I'd said 'yes please' before letting me know I'd have to play with a spring-loaded dart while I was over there this time.

With the notion of my having to get used to using spring-loaded darts in mind as per my conversation with Tony, I'll take a bit of time out here to talk about the types of darts that we play with and some of their quirks and differences in general as I am sure there will be some people reading this book who might think that one dart is pretty much like another. Sharp point at one end, plastic flight at the other. And, certainly as far as the sort of sets you might buy to mess about with in your garage, that's not so far from the truth. But there is a lot more to the dart than that.

The bit that you don't want to mess about with, the sharp bit at the front of a dart, is referred to as the point. There are two main types of dart point, the steel tip or the soft tip (which are more popular in the US and Europe) with the steel tip more likely to be the preference among the leading players. That's hardly surprising, though. Steel tips have been used since the early days of the game and for obvious reasons. For a start, they're heavier than their soft-tipped compatriots, which means you can be more sure of precision with your throw. A heavier dart is less likely to deviate from the course you have set it on from your hand to the board, and as that can be a throwing distance of around eight feet, it's important to know this. It also means they are strong and incredibly durable, so will be unlikely to bend or snap unless, if, in a fit of temper, you throw them against a hard surface. You might end up paying between £100–£150 for a decent set of tungsten steel darts, so you're getting quality for your money and should get a lot of use from them.

If the steel-tipped dart is the choice of the traditionalist then the plastic soft-tip dart is perhaps that of the player who is just coming into the game or for family use in and around the house, just as I used to in our kitchen with Mum and Dad. They might be looked down on a bit by the game's cognoscenti who all prefer the heavier steel tips but if someone wants to take up darts then I'd certainly recommend they start off with the softer, lighter variety, especially as they are a lot safer. Believe me, people ending up at their local A&E department as a result of being impaled by an errantly thrown dart, a risk that is significantly reduced if you are playing with soft-tip plastic darts. One clear advantage that the soft-tip darts have is that they are used on digital dartboards that keep the score for you as you throw, so they're ideal for those whose maths skills are maybe not as good as they'd like them to be.

The central part of a dart is referred to as the barrel, with the most common material used at present being nickel-tungsten. Tungsten barrels enable a dart to be very thin but still make the required weight. Look at some of the darts that Phil Taylor uses for example. They're very thin, so will fly through the air with little resistance, meaning Phil will know exactly where it is going to land on the board after he has thrown it. Back in the day, the barrel was made of brass, and these were a completely different animal, especially in the way they looked. Thick and chunky is a polite way of putting it, which didn't always lead to shooting a high score. In addition to that, brass isn't that durable either, so, even if the surface of the barrel had some sort of grip on it, constant use would soon start to wear this away.

There are a good few dart barrel types. One of the most popular is the straight barrel, used to great effect by Eric Bristow, who'd use their sleek lines to ease his darts past one another in pretty much the same part of the board – three straight-barrelled darts fit very nicely into the treble 20 bed. There is also the bomb barrel, a design that has been very popular for a long time now and which might best be described as 'short and fat'. These are similar to another type, the torpedo barrel, although these do have a bit of an edge, so to speak, as their weight is centred at the front of the barrel which means that when they hit the dartboard, the momentum that design gives them pretty much means they are going to stay put and not fall out.

I could go on. There are scallop barrels, which are meant to 'train' you to maintain the same grip every time you throw the dart, and tapered barrels, which are straight and quite thick at the front before they suddenly taper down along the stem. Finally, there is the stealth barrel, so called because it is tapered to a very thin diameter at both the front and rear of the barrel, meaning the experienced player should be able to squeeze his dart into a place on the board where you wouldn't normally expect them to even attempt a shot.

Right at the back of the dart is the flight. There are two common flight shapes, referred to as either standard or slim. Standard flight are used by most of the leading players as they're great for giving your dart stability in its flight path towards the dartboard, especially if you are the type of player who lobs your dart at the board rather than throwing it. There is a subtle difference, so take a look at some of the top players in action and see if you can see whether they lob or throw (or 'thrust' as it's also described) the dart at the board. Slim flights, on the other hand, are good if you like to throw the dart harder or if you prefer a lighter dart which means you have to throw with a little bit more force anyway. Their smaller size also means they are less likely to get damaged if they're all grouped together in the same place. There isn't, for example, much space left in the treble 20 bed when you've already got two in there and are going for the 180, so the more air, so to speak, there is between the two that are already in there, the better your chance of finding the space you need if your darts are all going to be close together.

When I first started playing league darts in Ipswich when I was 15, I was using a very light dart. I like the pear-shaped flight as well as a medium-sized stem. So the weight of my dart at the time was 15 grams, the same weight as one compact disc. So, as I said, very light. This suited me fine up until I was 18 and starting to play in the open tournaments. I was now under a lot more pressure to perform, play well and win, so I needed to play with a setup that suited both me and my game perfectly.

Darts wasn't 'just' a game anymore for me, and I found now that, if I was under pressure, I couldn't feel the weight of the dart. It was around about that time that, fortunately, the John Lowe dart had caught my eye so I gave them a go. They immediately felt right, suiting me a lot more and, crucially, they felt comfortable. They weighed 20 grams each (about the same weight as a mouse) which might not seem a huge difference and, of course, five grams isn't that much of a difference at all. But it was significant for me.

Marginal gains, fine margins. Well-used turns of phrase that apply in many competitive sports. This is where it became an applicable one for me.

When I was invited to play in three tournaments in the USA in 1981, a great opportunity that came along at exactly the right time, I'd previously found out, remember, that one of the 'requirements' of taking part was to use the newly introduced spring-loaded dart. With these, you have a barrel that then has a small spring and screw placed inside it; you then attach that, for want of a better word, 'pimped up' dart to a medium-sized stem and flight. These weighed only 21 grams, so the difference for me was negligible even if the dart I'd be using in America was going to be completely different to anything I'd used before. A good comparison, perhaps, was how leading tennis players were, around that time, having to adjust from the old wooden tennis rackets to the graphite ones they use today – which immediately made the wooden ones obsolete. That was all about power and control however, which wasn't the case with spring-loaded darts. Their advantage was supposed to come into play if you hit the wire on a dartboard. If that happened with a traditional dart, it would rebound off the board and count as a miss, but, with the spring-loaded ones, even if you hit a wire, the spring in the barrel would help it to stick in the board rather than fall off.

So someone wants me to play with a dart that I hadn't even heard of, let alone played with before. Well look. I'm a working-class lad from the Chantry Estate in Ipswich and, quite honestly, if it meant going to America for three weeks, I'd have thrown masonry nails at the dartboard, there was no way I was running any sort of risk of not going on that trip. As it turned out, the claims made about the spring-loaded dart and how it would 'stick', even if it hit the wire, didn't turn out to be at all accurate but, despite all that I won two of the events I was in out there and decided that I'd carry on using them which I did, including at the World Championship in 1983.

My first darts sponsor was Winmau, whose darts weighed in at 21 grams so that was perfect for me. After a few years with Winmau I moved on to a new company, Unicorn Darts, which remains one of the most respected names in the game. Interestingly enough, Unicorn owns Gunn & Moore, a name that any fan of cricket will be familiar with as the maker of some of the world's best cricket bats. Unicorn made my dart the same length as the ones I had previously been using with a pear-shaped flight. The weight, at 19 grams, was down a little on what I'd been using but I liked those darts very much and the partnership worked very well. Then, in 2007, I signed for Retriever Sports, a company which is not, in any way, as big a name in the sport as Winmau or Unicorn Darts, but the company not only made the length of my dart the same as that provided by my previous sponsors, but went on to provide a smaller stem which made my dart length overall a little bit shorter, something that suited me at the time.

Looking back as I write this, I realise that my dart likes or preferences haven't really changed all that much over the years. It's always been a case of knowing what I like and sticking with that formula throughout my career. That's all very different to the modern game where, for example, someone like Peter Wright can change the shape of his darts or the flights used on countless occasions. He's had specially designed darts made for him that change their colour depending on the light while, during the 2014 PDC World Championship, he was adjusting the weight, flight and stems of his darts, so much so that it looked as if he was changing them between rounds. But that's Peter for you, he has so much self-confidence and belief in his ability that he is able to carry it off.

I'm not so sure I could have done that.

Phil Taylor was also sponsored by Unicorn Darts. His sets would be identical and, more often than not, after he'd won a match or tournament, he'd give them away to some of the fans. After one world final, Phil got my daughter Lauren up on to the stage at the presentation and gave her the darts he won with. In addition to that, after he'd won a few other finals on television, he gave Matthew, my son, the winning darts. What a gentleman he is. A lot of players could never do this as they get used to the barrels, but Phil is such a genius of a darts player he can just unwrap a new set at any time and play with them as if he'd been using them all his life. We won't see another player like him for a long time, if ever. Phil can (and frequently does) do anything, and at times you can't help thinking that he could pick up any set of darts and win a world title with them.

There are players on the circuit today who are sponsored by one company but still go back to, and use, the darts they had from a previous sponsor which, for me, doesn't show any level of confidence in their setup. If you're not happy with the darts provided by your sponsor, then surely you should say so? I think the sponsor should be able, just as Target Darts (my manufacturer at the time) did with me, able to personalise them to your exact preferences. A lot of it will be, of course, down to self-confidence and getting used to a new set of darts though. Take Michael van Gerwen for example; he freely admitted at the end of 2020 that his last year or so in the game hadn't been a good one.

Michael had enjoyed a lot of success with some of his earlier sponsors but, as he had developed into a bigger and more well-known name in the game and his profile surged through the roof, he lost some of the form that had made him such a good player. It's all about having confidence and self-belief in your game, your darts and even your sponsors (and feeling that they have it with you as well), and this has applied to me in the past. You have to work hard to find it again if it happens, we can't all be complete naturals like Peter Wright who oozes self-belief. Happily for Michael, he proved that he'd found his darting mojo again when he won the 2020 Players Championship.

There is now so much money and commercial interest in the game that the deals, like the seven-year one Sky Sports signed with the PDC in 2017, will get bigger and bigger with more and more money involved. That means, as well as the massive interest in the game as a whole such deals and coverage provokes, there will also be more and more interest in the darts themselves: which players use what brands, the weights of their darts and even what materials are being used in manufacturing them. All of that sort of thing was completely unheard of in the 1970s and 1980s, when you found a dart that suited you and just kept using it until you either found another one you preferred, or if someone paid you enough money to switch over to their make. It happened, of course, but it didn't make the headlines as much as it has done with some of the examples of this happening in more recent years.

Changes and modifications to sporting equipment and all the endorsements that go with it are nothing new. I wrote earlier about how the world's leading tennis players had to adapt to using modern graphite rackets after nearly a century of playing with wooden ones. Now, more recently, there has been controversy about the US golfer Bryson DeChambeau breaking all sorts of distance records with his driver, and even going as far as experimenting with one that had a 48in-long shaft.

Darts equipment is still, for me, a pretty much straightforward thing. If you're considering changing or upgrading the darts you play with, then I'd say it all comes down to what weight suits your throw. So look at how hard you actually throw the dart in order to help you work out the ideal weight. If you don't put a lot of force behind your throw, then you may need a slightly heavier dart. Have a go, if you can, with a few different types and weights, trying, ideally, not to learn what it is before you throw one. Find out what feels right before finding out what weight it is.

As for the grip, for me, I don't feel the need for too much grip, so the grooves in my barrels are not too deep. I'd buy those small birthday candles that you use on cakes (I've bought so many, I must be about 200 years old now) and rub the wax on my barrels before putting chalk on top of it to ensure I had a smooth grip. It's a preference and method I've used throughout my career. Some of the top players, however, are always changing their grips or even the darts that they play with, but this usually happens when they're on a bit of a bad run and haven't been doing too well in the tournaments.

A player will always, believe me, blame their darts rather than themselves if they're on a bad run. I'm no exception either as, at the BDO World Championship in 1987, I lost 3-0 to Brian Cairns and was so disgusted at how I'd played that I ended up throwing my darts in the lake that the famous Lakeside venue is named after. It was my best throw all night.

Back to the story. I'm off to the USA again and I'm going to be playing with spring-loaded darts. It was all new to me but, like I've already said, nothing was going to stop me heading out there again and, having given Tony the answer he required with regard to the equipment I'd be using, we headed off over the pond once more.

The first event that Tony and I appeared in was being held at Lake Tahoe in California. We might, I guess, have been wondering how the Lake Tahoe 'crowd' might have taken to darts. It is, after all, a major tourist attraction that plays host to a variety of winter sports as well as many other forms of outdoor summer recreation. California is, after all, and unsurprisingly when you consider its favourable climate, a state that loves physical exercise and all sorts of outdoor activities. So how were they going to take to darts?

We weren't disappointed and it turned out that they loved the game, especially as I got to the final of that particular tournament, only to lose to Chicago-born Dan Pucillo. Dan's darts story is one that needs to be mentioned here. He was, so the story goes, working in a managerial capacity at an import/export company where the stress and pressures of the job were starting to give him ulcers. So, one day, he decided to close his office door and put a dartboard on the back of it, the sort of stress release and all-round communal bit of fun that companies all around the world like to have in their office or warehouses. Things turned out rather unexpectedly for Dan, however, as it transpired that he was rather good – good enough, as it turned out, to win the US national championships three times before travelling overseas to play on the professional circuit, as well as beating the occasional Brit who came over to play him in his own backyard.

I might have lost to Dan, but at least I'd made the final so, all in all, Lake Tahoe had been a good start to the tour which greatly encouraged Tony and I as we made our way to our second destination, the Austin Open in Texas. We had a bit of time to spare though so, en route, we stopped off at a place in Albuquerque to play in an event there. This time it was an all-British affair in the final as Tony and I made our way through the field and, just as I'd hoped after Lake Tahoe, I went one step further and beat him in the final. We then took up a kind invitation from a guy who was at the tournament to stay the night at his house before making our way to Austin the next day, a modest little trip (by US standards anyway) of around 700 miles.

He seemed an okay guy. He'd done well in life as he drove a Porsche, but I was more than a little unnerved by the fact that he had a pet rattlesnake in the house with him. Tony wasn't so bothered mind you, as he only had eyes for this guy's Porsche which he eventually got into and took out for a spin in the surrounding desert. Plenty of room you might think, no danger of him hitting something out there. Wrong. I'd tried to stop him from heading off as the car was a bit of a beast and you need to be a bit of one yourself to handle such a powerful car. But he insisted, just as I insisted on not going out there with him.

Off he went and, sure enough, he ended up having a terrible crash out in the desert that left him with a big gaping hole in the back of his head. Luckily for Tony, a doctor was driving back to the town and was in that same part of the desert (what are the odds?) so he was able to give Tony some immediate medical attention before getting him off to the local hospital. The Porsche didn't fare quite so well as its back was crushed so badly that anyone who'd been sitting there at the time of the accident would have had absolutely no chance of survival.

So I had to head off to Austin to play in the tournament there without my mate and wingman. I played well though and ended up getting a little bit of revenge on Dan Pucillo by beating him in the final. It was one of those evenings really with one of the highlights, so to speak, for me happening while I was throwing some darts at the practice board beforehand when someone shouted over to me asking if I wanted some coke?

'No thanks,' I replied. 'But I'd love a beer.'

Except he wasn't offering me the soft drink, he was asking me if I fancied some cocaine. That was me all over, Mr Naive from deepest Suffolk. This was all changing now, I was living and playing in a different world and nothing illustrated it better than that short little exchange.

The final event of the tour was also the biggest of the three. This was the grandly titled Cleveland Extravaganza, which was going to be broadcast on live television. I played well and got to the final where I was due to meet Jerry Umberger, who was the USA number one at the time. Jerry wasn't totally unknown as a player, having competed in the BDO World Darts Championship that year and, although he wasn't seeded, he beat another North American player, Len Heard (who was seeded 12), in the first round before going out to Cliff Lazarenko in the second round. So he played to a decent standard and I knew it would be a tough match. Fortunately, no one offered me any drugs prior to the final, and I was able to see off Jerry, meaning that at the tour's conclusion I was now up by about $10,000, which wasn't a bad result at all. I gave Tony half of that amount after being told by the sponsors that I could keep the money, even though Tony hadn't been able to complete the tour. He was delighted as his misadventures in the Porsche had meant him missing out on two of the three tournaments we were due to play in together but we had agreed to split any winnings we got between us before we went out there, and I was delighted to still do this and put a smile on Tony's face at the end of the tour.

Later that year I won two more tournaments back in the UK. These were important ones for me as, because players from all over the country were entering them, it meant the quality of opposition I was competing against was higher than it had been when I was focusing on the circuit in and around East Anglia. The first one I won was the Hastings Open, which had a first prize of £400. I then went on to play in a tournament that was very close to home – the Suffolk Open, which was held in Ipswich. I really wanted to win this one as you might have guessed, local boy and all that, and I managed to do so, although it was tough as I had to beat Charlie Ellix, an England international, in the semi-final before coming up against Mick Norris in the final. I won that with a 120 finish while Mick was sitting on double top to win. He won the News of the World Championship in 1977, so it was really pleasing for me to not only beat a top-ranked player but to do so in my home town.

While I was back in the USA to play in the North American Open, I'd come down with a bit of a sore throat. By the following day, when I was due to play in three different events, I was beginning to feel rather unwell as the pain in my throat steadily got worse. I was due to play in the singles tournament on the Sunday morning and had thought, perhaps naively, that a good night's sleep would shake it off once and for all and I'd be good to play in that. If only. I headed downstairs from my hotel room in order to practise at 9.30am (the singles was due to start at 11am) and, by then, I could hardly speak. So I now had to acknowledge that something was wrong with me.

But I still wanted to play. I'd travelled a long way to do so and had fancied my chances of doing well in a field of 512 players which meant you had to play and win eight rounds in order to reach the final. Mind you, it was brutal stuff – it was first to 301, rather than 501, and the winner was the first to win two out of three games. So you could head all the way out there only to have to come home again very quickly indeed.

I was up against John Lowe and John could see that I was unwell. He won 2-0 and that was it for me so I went straight back to my room, which I was sharing with Denis Ovens, and went to bed, determined to stay there until the next day, when we were all flying back to England. I told Denis what I was going to do and, top man that he is, he popped back to the room a few hours later just to see how I was. It's just as well he did as all I could do was hand him a piece of paper on which I'd written, 'Please get me to the hospital.'

Once we got there and I'd handed over $150, a doctor saw me. He told me that I had an abscess which was getting bigger and steadily making its way towards my windpipe. He promptly cut it out, resulting in a stream of red pus oozing from where it had been. Which wasn't very nice. But it made an almost instantaneous difference to me, although he curtailed my relief somewhat by commenting that it was just as well I'd come to see him on that day as, if I'd have started the flight home on the next one, I would not have survived as I would have choked to death.

Denis has never forgotten this and, whenever we see one another, he always reminds me about how he saved my life.

I'm now recalling another trip to the USA (I was quite the globetrotter in those days) which was undertaken in order to play in the North American Open, once again in Las Vegas. The event sponsor that year was Ken Kercheval, who'd played the part of Cliff Barnes in the popular US soap *Dallas*. As well as acting, Ken also had his own popcorn business but he was very fond of his darts, despite all his other distractions, and was, as a result, good friends with Tom Fleetwood, who ran the American Darts Organisation. Tom had played the barman in the *High Chaparral* TV show, as well as appearing in *Dallas* and, as Ken introduced me to him, I couldn't help thinking how strange it was that I was now here, working alongside and socialising with two people whose faces were so familiar to us as fans of both shows back in England.

My trips to the USA were always eventful but I learned a lot from them, and not just about darts but life as well. But 1982 was now fast approaching. I was playing well, winning tournaments and getting a bit of a name for myself. It wouldn't be long, I was told, before I'd be selected to play for England, the ultimate sporting honour for any English man or woman, whatever your event was. I just had to make sure that I kept playing consistently well for my county, kept my averages up and make sure that I was one of the players who was constantly noticed.

It was time to move up a gear or two and look to become the leading character in my own soap opera.

3

World Affairs

This was, make no mistake,
a massive step up for me.

SOMETHING THAT had been duly noted as far as Keith
Deller was concerned was how well my 'mini-tour' of the USA
had gone during the following summer of 1982. I'd won one
of the events, beating Bobby George, Bob Anderson and John
Lowe on my way to the final before getting past Denis Ovens
(a nice way to thank him for saving my life last time we were
out there) in the final.

The US-based events were always well attended and
organised and I'd played well in getting to the finals of all three
of the ones we'd gone to, winning one more in addition to the
one mentioned above and had, in the process, generated more
than a little bit of interest in darts over the pond, especially as
a limey who'd dared to go over there and beat a couple of their
best players. Most Americans believe that their sports teams

and individuals are, by default, the best in the world so the word was out that they wanted me to head out there again in order for them to have a little bit of revenge and to set things straight.

It more than suited me to head off over there once again. I'd enjoyed our previous trip enormously, other than, of course, Tony's excursion in the Porsche. I even managed to get myself a little bit of extra pocket money prior to flying out there as, the night before my flight, I went for a curry with John Markovic and Linda Batten at their local curry house in Enfield. It turned out to be quite a night really as a few of the other top players of the time came along as well so the banter ended up flowing as freely as the pints of lager.

We'd been discussing some of the dishes on the menu and, as a load of lads will tend to do when they go out for a curry, the talk turned to what the hottest item on there might have been. Anyway, after a few exchanges, it was decided that if I could eat the hottest one (it was probably a phaal) they'd all give me £50 which would, considering how many of them were there, have been quite a tidy sum for me to have in my pocket. The dish in question was duly ordered and my God, it was unbelievably hot, but, somehow, I managed to get through it and went back to John and Linda's that night with a nice little bonus.

I thought I'd come out of it all rather well but fate caught up with me the next day as I proceeded to spend around half of the 11-hour flight out to Los Angeles in the plane toilet, much to the amusement of everyone else. I had, fortunately, enough time to recover before the tournament, which I won.

This meant, as I found out shortly afterwards, I'd now receive an invitation to play in the qualifiers for the following year's World Championship which the British Darts Organisation (BDO) had, given the number of players who now wanted to take part in it, decided to introduce for the 1983 tournament onwards.

This was, make no mistake, a massive step up for me.

I'd enjoyed the trips over to the USA and had enjoyed the successes I'd had there. It had been good fun as well as a massive learning experience – about darts, about the tour and about life in general. I was, remember, just 23 years old as 1982 drew to a close, a relative youngster still, especially in the game itself, one whose greatest exponents had usually found fame and glory heading their way when they were a lot older. I was breaking the mould already but I wanted more now and, far from being overawed at the prospect of playing in the worlds, I felt I ought to go into it thinking that I had as good a chance as anyone of winning – even if I was probably the only person who was thinking that way at the time. I was known in the game and I'd played all of the big names, they respected me of course as a fellow professional but did any of them believe I was capable of moving up several steps and being a potential world champion? Whatever they'd previously thought, I'd now have the chance to show them I could do just that.

Was I nervous? I don't think so, not particularly. I had a lot of faith in myself so, if anything, I was confident rather than nervous and, as we headed down to London for the qualifiers, Linda Batten was spending most of her time just trying to keep me calm and focused on the matches ahead. She knew that it was one thing being confident of your chances, but you can take things a little bit too far and that is when confidence becomes complacency, so she worked hard on bringing me back down to earth whenever it might have looked as if I was losing a little bit of that focus.

My first qualifying game was against a player from Spain. I'd been to the country and had never seen a dartboard there, not once, so it came as a bit of a surprise to me to learn that someone there was not only playing the game but was considered good enough to be asked to fly over to London to compete at this level. Anyway, decent enough lad that he was, he wasn't up to my standard and I won 9-0, a perfect start for me and one that perfectly prepared me for what would, undoubtedly, be a few tougher games to come. And it couldn't have come much harder than my second-round opponent at the qualifiers, a player called Len Heard, who John and Linda both knew very well. He was the man who, if you'll recall, got to the final of the 1978 North American Open before being beaten by Bobby George. Len would therefore be a lot tougher an opponent than the Spanish no-hoper I'd come across in the previous round and, given that Len was 40 and had been playing darts since he was 18, he certainly wasn't lacking in experience either, including at the worlds where he'd competed in 1980, losing to Dave Whitcombe in the first round. Linda knew all about that and she knew that Len was a good player who was more than capable of getting through the qualifiers, so she urged me not to underestimate him, but there was never any danger of me doing that and I ended up winning that match 9-1.

Two down, one to go and only one game lost. I was on a roll. My opponent for the last qualifying round was Jim McGuigan who was, at the time, the number two-ranked player in Scotland. So, again, a potentially difficult match in prospect for me but, by now, I was riding the momentum gained from my first two victories and ended up going into this final game knowing I'd win. This wasn't arrogance. I was just so confident by then; I'd played really well in the previous two rounds and had, as far as most people would have been concerned, knocked out one of the favourites in the qualifiers when I'd beaten Len. I ended up beating Jim 9-0, another convincing victory, and against a good player, an overall performance which would, I'd hoped, make my name a little bit more familiar within the game.

There was no time for celebrating though. I was through and all set to make my World Championships debut at the Jollees Cabaret Club in Stoke-on-Trent, which had been hosting the event since 1979 when John Lowe had defeated Leighton Rees in the final. The total prize money on offer for the whole tournament back then was £15,000, of which £4,500 went to John and £2,000 to Leighton. Now, four years later, the total on offer had been raised to £33,050, with £8,000 going to the winner. It was, even back then, hardly a life-changing amount of money to win (John McEnroe got £66,600 for winning Wimbledon that year while Steve Davis won £30,000 for winning the World Snooker Championship) but it was, nevertheless, more money than I'd ever seen or even come close to winning before. Mind you, to be honest, the prize money could have been £1, £1,000, or even £1m – the amount on offer didn't really matter to me as much as the prestige and honour of winning the tournament would have done.

One of the first people I met when I arrived at the venue was Peter Purves, the former *Blue Peter* presenter who made that comment about me being the top qualifier out of the four who'd made it through from London a few weeks earlier. I'm sure that, and as per my thoughts earlier in this book, he expected me to respond by saying how honoured I was to be there and that I was just going to enjoy myself and the occasion. It was the sort of comment you might expect from the manager of a non-league football team if they've been drawn to play at somewhere like Liverpool or Manchester City in an FA Cup tie; the familiar refrain of someone who knew their place, so to speak, in the sporting order of things.

But I wasn't thinking along those lines. I'd just come through a tough qualifying tournament having won my three matches by an aggregate score of 27-1. I'd already played against, and beaten, some of the sport's biggest names, including being part of the team who'd beaten the one containing Eric Bristow and John Lowe at the North American Open as well as, in my younger days, beating Eric, much to his surprise, at one of the regular darts nights we'd hold at my local when I was just 17 so he, at least, knew what I was all about and capable of, even if Peter Purves didn't. So I wanted to put Peter right, hence my response to him of, 'I am better than that, I will be world champion at the end of the week.' Confident? Definitely. Cocky? Maybe a little. But, more than that, I had so much belief in my ability and knew I was capable of winning if I played well. Peter certainly picked up on that confidence, putting £20 on me at 66/1 as a result of our meeting. He'd end up nearly £1,500 better off by the end of the tournament as a result of that bet – and he didn't forget either, as he bought me a magnum of champagne at the end of the year when we all got together to celebrate the tenth birthday of the BDO.

I'd been drawn to play Nicky Virachkul in the first round. I'd played, and beaten Nicky quite a few times a year earlier if you remember; he'd been one of the players who'd popped into The Rising Sun for a bit of pre-tournament practice, so, in a way, it was an ideal match-up for me as I knew him and was familiar with his game. I don't know if he remembered me or not, but, regardless of that, he'd have found out a little bit about me by now and would certainly have known I was one of the qualifiers which might, in a way, have made him even more focused for our match than he might normally have been, as he wouldn't have wanted to go out in the first round against someone who's come through qualifying. So I wanted to be ready for him and, on the day of our match, I was up for breakfast at 6am before going over to the practice room by 7am, spending the next three hours in there. I was the only one in there and might have stayed put right up to the time Nicky and I were due to play, had it not been for Linda telling me that she didn't want me on stage later on having left all of my great darts in the practice room. So, by 10am, I was back in my room chilling out and getting myself mentally prepared, knowing that, as far as putting in the practice was concerned, I'd done everything I possibly could.

John and Linda knocked on my door at 11.30am and we all made our way over to the venue. Up until then, I'd been calm and was just looking forward to getting up on the stage but, as I started to take note of all the people milling around the place, that and the TV people and all their equipment and the trucks that it came in, I started to get a little nervous. It didn't help that I had to do an interview for the BBC just before we were due up but I got through that without any slip-ups although, again, I was very aware of the TV cameras, lights and cables that were strewn about all over the place. I'd never played on TV before while Nicky had, so, at that stage at least, the psychological advantage was probably with him. It was absolutely vital, therefore, that I got off to a good start and I did, winning the first set before Nicky, great professional that he was, came back to win the second, making the score 1-1.

The momentum was now in his favour and, at that stage, he might, again, have thought the psychological advantage was with him.

Looking back, that final set is probably one of the most important, in terms of my career, that I've ever played. Yes, it was the BDO World Darts Championship but this was still the first round and, even if Nicky was the seventh seed, he was still pretty much an unknown as far as most darts fans were concerned. Other first-round matches that year saw Eric beat Peter Masson and John Lowe (with a three-dart average of 97.20) see off Alan Evans, while Jocky Wilson eased into the second round by beating Steve Brennan, who'd caused a bit of a sensation a year earlier by knocking out Eric in the first round. So, all things considered, my match against Nicky was, in boxing terms, one that might have featured on the undercard. Had I lost it I'd have been making my way home, still an unknown, and would have had to go through qualifying again if I was to be one of the players at the BDO a year later. Sink or swim? Not quite. But from a career point of view, dipping out so early on in my first worlds wouldn't have been ideal.

That was motivation enough. I think, at that stage, I wanted the win more than Nicky did; maybe there was more at stake for me and that translated into my darts over that final leg, which never really saw me in any danger of losing as I won it 3-0. I now had a day off before my next match and vowed to spend it getting as much practice in as possible as I didn't want to undo all the good work I'd done in beating Nicky by letting myself down in the second round.

I was up to play Les Capewell, a local lad who would be guaranteed great support. He, like Nicky, wasn't a big name in the game, so I would, again, be playing on the tournament's undercard but, for all that, Les had qualified for the worlds in each of the previous two years, even though he'd failed to get past the first round. He'd now put that right by beating Stuart Holden so would, rightfully, have been fairly confident of seeing me off and getting a place in the last eight which might have meant a chance of being in the spotlight by playing John Lowe in the quarter-finals, something that Les, and his large and vocal group of supporters, would have relished as both they and he would have fancied their chances by then. There was also added pressure in the fact that whoever won the match between us was guaranteed a place in the next World Championship – so there was quite a lot to play for already by that stage.

I could liken it to your favourite football team getting to the FA Cup quarter-finals. Once you get to the last eight, you start to dream of a sunny May afternoon (or evening as it is now) at Wembley and believe that this might just be your year and that you can go all the way. Ipswich got that far in 1978. Liverpool and Manchester United were out, and, although Nottingham Forest (who were a very good side at the time) and Arsenal were both in the competition at that stage, we avoided both and were drawn to play against Millwall. They were in the Second Division (now the Championship) at the time, so were a team we knew we could beat – which we did, 6-1 – and that doing so would mean we'd be just one game from the final. That logic would have been foremost in the minds of Les and his supporters – beat Deller and end up playing either John or Terry O'Dea for a place in the last four. You can't help but get excited and think that your time in the sun has arrived and the noise his fans were making suggested exactly that. The only problem with that was that I wasn't, as Millwall might have been on that day five years earlier, just happy to be there; I felt the draw was opening up for me as well and won 3-1. To be fair to Les's fans, they gave me a lot of respect throughout the match and it was played in a good spirit throughout.

I averaged 94.20, a total that was only beaten, inevitably, by Eric who averaged 96.00 in his win over Dave Lee. Dave had made a game of it though and Eric had won 3-2, an indication, maybe, that he wasn't, at that early stage, playing his best darts. But I knew that all the great champions build up their game and momentum as a tournament progresses and Eric would have been confident of getting to the final. The way the draw had been structured meant that we wouldn't be able to play each other until the final and that suited me as, if you want to be a champion, you've got to prove yourself by playing against the very best and beating them en route. It's no good hoping so-and-so gets knocked out early so you don't have to play him, and I certainly wasn't wishing for early departures for Eric, John or Jocky at all. If I was to win, I wanted to beat them all and I now had the chance to do so, as John had seen off Terry and would be waiting for me in the quarter-final, which just about everyone, apart from me, was tipping him to win.

I'd watched John's game against Terry and, for me, he'd been fortunate to win it in the end. John had won the BDO in 1979 and had also made the last two finals, losing to Eric in 1981 and Jocky in 1982. There was no doubt, in my mind, that John had another World Championship in him. He was a wonderful player in his prime and he could, like Eric, have been playing himself into the tournament and was now ready, with just three opponents left, one of whom was a qualifier. So he'd be ready to hit his peak.

* * *

I'd been confident of beating Nicky and Les as I believed that I was their equal, but John was a major step up in quality as far as an opponent was concerned, and, although I still had the belief, I also knew I was going to have to play one of the matches of my life to beat him, especially as the pressure was now on a little bit – people were beginning to take notice of me and I was starting to make the headlines in the sports news. This was going to be the biggest match of my life so far. I just hoped that two even bigger ones would quickly follow.

My quarter-final against John was played two days after my victory over Les. I hadn't spent much of that time taking it easy. Even if I went over to Jollees to take a look at some of the other matches, I was always trying to work out how each of the players were thinking, the shots they were playing (or the ones they weren't) as well as how they appeared to be up on the stage – relaxed, tense, a bit uptight, whether they were smiling or not, all of that sort of thing. I wanted to make the very most of the opportunity I had and not waste even a second of it on stuff that had nothing to do with darts. I was about to play in the quarter-finals of the biggest tournament in the sport, it would be shown on TV and, as it was due to be played on the evening of 6 January, the crowd, many of whom would be John's supporters, would have had a whole day to relax, enjoy themselves and sink back a few beers in the process.

On the afternoon of the match, I put in a solid four hours of practice back at the hotel. If I lost to John, then I did not want to look back at any part of my preparation and wonder if things might have turned out differently; for example, if I'd practiced more or spent less time relaxing in my room. Linda Batten had told me more than once not to leave my best darts in the practice room and she had a point. There was a fine line between not taking my preparation seriously enough or, on the other hand, putting so much attention and focus into it that I found myself with little to nothing to give when the match started.

Ultimately, I think I got the balance right and it showed early on as I got off to a perfect start, taking a 2-0 lead and playing as well as I had done in the tournament so far. I was halfway there and, maybe, at that stage, some players might have mentally given up the fight and left me an easy route to victory, a 4-1 maybe, or even a 4-0. But we're talking about John Lowe here, one of the greatest names to have ever played darts and, at 2-0, he clicked, and, to pinch Linda's saying, he began to find his best form. He won the third set and the fourth, which brought the score to 2-2, before taking the fifth to go 3-2 up. This meant I was now just one set from going out of the championship. By now, I suspect, people at the venue as well as those watching back home on TV would have been thinking John would push on and win the match 4-2, adding that the 'unknown' from Suffolk had enjoyed his moment in the sun and 'hadn't he done well?', but it was now time for this particular sporting fairytale to end.

It was a battle now, one in which holding your nerve was as important as shooting a good score. It's all too easy to miss what commentators might call an 'easy shot' when the pressure is on and we've all seen it – someone has needed a double top to win a match and missed it with all three of their darts. Golf is famous for its 'yips', that sporting affliction that has affected some of its greatest players who find, after being successful for year after year, they can barely grip their putter, let alone play a shot with it. Is there an equivalent in darts? You may have heard of 'dartitis', the name given to the nervous twitching or tension that can affect a player's concentration and, as a result, affect performance. There is no, as far as we know, physical reason for this to crop up and interfere with your game; it's seen as purely a mental block which means you can struggle to even release your dart, let alone shoot the score you want. It had never affected me before but, as I stood there, 3-2 down and possibly making my exit from the tournament, I felt, for maybe the first time in my career, the sort of pressure, most of which was self-inflicted in my case, that affects elite sportsmen and women all over the world.

* * *

As we prepared for the sixth set, I knew I was about to play the most important legs of darts of my life. John was used to the pressure and expectation that came with being a world champion as he'd been there before, soaked it all up and emerged as the winner on countless occasions. But he hadn't been in that position with me before. Perhaps, and only perhaps, the fact I was still a bit of an unknown made him over-analyse the game a bit more than he needed to and his performance slipped just a little. He might also have given it his all to recover from 2-0 down and go 3-2 up so maybe he'd peaked during his comeback? Or, and stuff all this analysis, we were just two good darts players putting on a bit of a show for a packed crowd – there is, after all, a tendency in us all to over-analyse things.

All I knew at that stage was how desperate I was to win. It showed. I won the sixth set 3-0, surprising, I think, everyone by playing some great darts in the process and not wasting any opportunities to see a game out, so it was 3-3 and winner takes all. Who'd hold their nerve?

I edged it at the beginning of the final set and went 2-0 up, checking out on 127 with 20, treble 19 and a bullseye, leading to the BBC's commentator, the legend that was Sid Waddell to remark, 'The kid from Suffolk, who came not just to do well, but to win' – clearly Peter Purves had already had a word with Sid. It was, as another famous sports commentator later said, 'up for grabs now' as I was just one leg away from victory, a great position to be in – and yes, if I'd been convincing myself that I was handling the pressure up to this point then maybe I was now really beginning to feel it. The match was nip and tuck all the way now, with the scoring (mine first) as follows: 140-140; 100-60; 60-100; 60-40 (John had a bounce-out with his last dart on that visit, hence the lower score), and, finally, 89-45. That left John needing 161 to win the game and, with it, the match, but he threw 20, five and 20, meaning he still needed to score 116 to pull me back to 2-1 ahead in legs in my favour – but, crucially, I was already on 52 and it was now my throw.

Focus Keith. Twelve and double top gets you a place in the semi-final.

Twelve.

'He wants double top.' Sid again.

Throw. Miss. A fraction too high.

Re-adjust. Come on Keith, you've been hitting double tops since you were at school. You can hit them in your sleep. You need this one because John will check out on 116. Don't let him in.

I don't think Jollees had ever been so quiet.

Double top. I've done it. I'm in the semi-finals.

I couldn't help but do a little jump for joy. It had been a great match, a tense one at the end but also one which, I hope, entertained everyone who was watching. John took it like the pro he is, congratulating me and then, while I quickly left the stage, he stayed put and finished his drink like he'd just lost a friendly game at his local rather than the quarter-final of the World Championship.

I didn't have to wait too long for the semi-final, which would be against Jocky. He'd breezed his way past Cliff Lazarenko in his quarter-final and was now the hot favourite to see me off and set up, in the process, what most people would have thought of as the 'dream' final. Jocky against Eric, or, more importantly, Scotland against England, and everything that went with that.

Except that my support, which had been purely local at the beginning of the tournament, was now become something of a national issue as everyone was talking about 'the kid from Suffolk' and whether or not he could continue his rise from rural obscurity and, as a qualifier – someone who, in effect, was only there to make up the numbers – get all the way to the final.

I prepared for the match in pretty much the same way I had before I played John: four hours of practice at the hotel followed by a few hours' peace and quiet in my room. John and Linda had then arranged for us all to meet for a meal at 2pm before going over to the venue a couple of hours later and, first and foremost, getting all of the TV, radio and newspaper interviews out of the way before focusing on what was to come. Jocky was a great player and a fierce competitor, so never mind a potential final with Eric being Scotland versus England, he'd have seen his match with me in exactly the same way and that would have been enough to fire him up. He was the reigning champion and had earned that in some style a year earlier, beating Rab Smith, Alan Evans, Dave Miller and Stefan Lord, dropping just one set on the way, before beating John in the final.

Eric, the defending champion, make a very surprising exit at the first round stage, losing 2-0 to Steve Brennan, so there might have been some people wondering whether Jocky would still have won it that year had Eric stayed in and got all the way to the final. Jocky now had the perfect opportunity to win it for the second year running and by beating Eric in the final, so if anyone had doubted (foolishly, I might add) his winning credentials in 1982, he was now very well placed to prove them wrong.

Was it too much to expect to get off to a great start in this match as well? I'd started all of my previous rounds really quickly, hitting high scores and, in the process, proving Linda that I wasn't, as she'd feared, leaving the best part of my game in the practice room. Jocky was a difficult opponent to have in any tournament and at any stage. He breathed darts in the same way a dragon did fire and there was no way, as far as he was concerned, that he, the reigning world champion, was going to concede his hard-earned crown. So it wasn't a case of hoping to get off to a flying start, I *had* to, it was as simple as that. Because if I didn't, Jocky would wave me goodnight. He'd only dropped one set in his run to the semi-finals in 1982 and, at that stage, had beaten Stefan Lord 4-0. Phenomenal darts. So a great start was essential now rather than desirable. Jocky simply didn't do 'nip and tuck', if he went ahead then, more often than not, that was it, game over.

Job done, then. I won the first set during which, in the third leg, Jocky missed a double 18 that would, if he'd got it, have given him a perfect nine-dart leg. This is the darting equivalent of making a maximum 147 break in snooker and is so unusual that, at that time, nobody had done it on TV before. More to the point for Jocky, if he had hit that double 18 and checked out, he'd have won £52,000, which was nearly seven times the amount that the eventual winner would have got. Clearly, the sponsors thought their money was safe but Jocky came so close to taking it from them. I must have been the only person in Jollies who was delighted that he didn't, although I did, of course, feel for him as well.

Jocky still got back to 1-1 and we ended up sharing the next four sets, meaning the match was tied at 3-3 and could quite easily have gone either way. It was the best of nine at this stage meaning that even if I lost the seventh set and went 4-3 down, I'd still be in with a chance but Jocky would know he needed to win just one of the two remaining sets to get into the final. That was a feeling I wanted to have and, playing with as much focus as I think I'd ever had up until then, I won the seventh set 3-1 to go 4-3 up and find myself just one set away from the final. It had been, contrary to what I've written earlier, nip and tuck after all. Jocky had seen out the first leg with a double 16 while I was stuck on needing double one, the elusive score that everyone who plays the game for fun hates having to check out on.

Jocky threw his double 16 with his first dart, as I knew he would, and it was advantage Scotland.

I had wondered, albeit briefly, if missing that double 18 earlier on had affected Jocky. I know it would have played on my mind. It wasn't so often that you got the chance to throw one dart, just one dart, into part of the board you could normally hit without thinking and end up winning £52,000. He'd done all the hard work getting there only to miss out right at the end. It must have hurt. But, despite missing out, he continued to look calm and composed, as if he was having a friendly match with some of his mates up at the Alpha Bar in Fife where he fine-tuned his game and set himself on the way to being a world champion.

Jocky opened the second leg with 140. He was on fire now and looking for a quick win to even up the match. That would mean we had to go to a deciding set. He'd be very confident of winning that one as well, having been there before, and would have reckoned he had the game and the experience to beat me at that stage. He might have been right as well. I needed some great darts and I needed them now.

180. If he thought I was about to crumble in the heat of the action, he'd thought wrong.

Jocky was still playing well though and ended up needing 101 to take a 2-0 lead in legs in the eighth set. One of the traditional checkouts for that score is treble 20, single nine and double 16, and Jocky went for the treble 20 with his first dart but just missed, scoring 20 and leaving himself 81, his favourite shot, to win.

He needed treble 15, leaving double 18 to win. He duly nailed the treble but, on the cusp of taking that 2-0 lead, scored 18, meaning he was still 18 short and needed double nine. It was, I knew straight away, an opening that I had to take. I was on 123, not the easiest of checkouts as it meant I had to make every dart count.

Single 19. Treble 18. Bull to win.

Yes; 1-1 in legs.

It wasn't as if I'd suspected the match would be anything other than a battle, but those two tense opening legs had more than confirmed it. Neither of us had been at anything like 100 per cent but, if there had been any nerves, the fact we'd both won one leg and got things going would have helped dissipate them.

You couldn't really have picked a winner from the next four legs. It was tight, some good darts, some not so good darts, from both of us. The crowd, naturally, loved it, even if we both had a lot of partisan support there that night. Jocky's were as noisy and boisterous as you'd expect and, at times, it felt a bit like we were in a football match. As far as the game of darts was concerned, that was great. The TV coverage it was getting back then, remember, was still fairly minimal while the BBC's coverage was led by Peter Purves, who was hardly renowned as a sports presenter. He'd only left *Blue Peter* four years earlier and some people might have been wondering if the BBC was wondering quite what to do with him. He'd fronted a couple of children's shows that had a sporting theme as well as being part of its Crufts coverage and the main presenter of a motorcycling show called *Kick Start*. He was now the main presenter for darts and, while he was good at his job, it wasn't like he was a David Coleman, Richie Benaud or Peter Alliss. The BBC must have been pleased with him, though, as he retained his links with the sport for around seven years but, for all that, I still believe that the 1982 BDO World Championship was one of the events that made the BBC, as well as other broadcasters, realise that darts was about to take off in a big way and that its coverage would have to be treated in much the same way as football, cricket or golf if it was to remain on its channels.

Jocky and I were certainly doing our bit by putting on a show for the evening audience sat on their sofa.

With the score 4-3 in sets in my favour and with me 2-1 up after three legs, I made the perfect start to the next leg, hitting a 180. Then, as Jocky went to respond, he was disrupted by someone in the crowd who'd said something at the wrong moment, which was enough to snap Jocky out of his rhythm so much that he turned and said something back to them.

It wasn't something anyone wanted to see at the end of what had been a great match, and I didn't want to win because someone had put Jocky off (he'd only thrown 15) but I now had as good a chance as I would ever have to get to a world final, so I had to put that little incident right out of my mind and just concentrate on my own darts.

To the credit of Jocky's fans, not one of them tried to put me off in return and I threw 100 then another 100 to leave myself needing 121 to win. Jocky had, I think, 'gone' by then; he looked rattled and it seemed as if he just wanted the match to finish and to get off the stage and out of Jollies. I checked out on 121 (treble 20, treble 15 and double eight) to win the set and match, much to, I am sure, the surprise of most of the people watching who'd expected Jocky to win and set up what some might have considered that 'dream' final against Eric Bristow.

Jocky was interviewed by Peter Purves shortly after the game and, sportsman that he is, he said some very nice things about me in response to Peter asking him about playing in such a 'good game of darts' and still losing.

'I've told you all week. I've been practising with Keith … he's played bloody marvellous all week. He's a great player, he's come through well – he had to qualify for the event and I think he's a tremendous player.

'I know Keith from years past. I've played with him in America … he's a nice gentleman. It's a bit sick losing to him but I think he'll go on to win the championship.'

Peter then pointed out that I was, for most people, an 'unknown quantity'. Jocky, to his eternal credit, soon put him right at the same time while, it has to be said, rather undermining Peter's credibility as a darts presenter.

'Can I say something? He's *not* an unknown quantity. As far as the viewers are concerned, he is but, for the top professional players, Keith Deller is always there, no matter where we go in the world.'

He didn't have to say any of that. He was the reigning champion who had just been knocked out in the semi-finals. That's a stage at any elite contest level, no matter what the sport, where you don't want to lose. To get so far, to raise your hopes, week by week or, as it was for us, day by day, only to lose at the last minute and not make the final. It hurts. People often say the sense of disappointment at losing a major final can be cushioned by at least having the consolation of knowing that you'd got there and had a chance to enjoy the moment and the event itself. But losing a semi-final? There's nothing to be said that could possibly be good about that. Yet, having gone through it himself, Jocky made sure his post-match interview wasn't about him but was about me.

A true sportsman and a great professional – even if he then put the pressure on by saying he thought I'd beat Eric in the final!

Eric Bristow. The number one seed and the favourite to win it from the start. Nothing about that was going to change now.

But I was ready.

4

138 – Game, Shot and the Match

The first set is, for me, as important
as any you'll play in a match

Saturday, 8 January 1983

We were barely a week into a new year and, already, one of the biggest sporting days of 1983 was upon us, which would have millions of people licking their lips in delighted anticipation of an underdog taking on one of the big names in sporting conflict, taking them and having every chance of beating them, even if they'd come through a host of qualifying rounds just to reach the much hallowed stage they were now at. It was their day in the sun, their 15 minutes of fame.

But the romance of their run into the limelight was about to come to an end at the hands of one of the game's big guns, a known winner and familiar name to sporting fans across the globe.

Eric Bristow, Keith Deller and BDO World Championship Final day then? No, have a word with yourself. I'm talking about the FA Cup third round. The FA Cup remains, for me, the biggest and best football competition there is. There's nothing quite like it. I'd enjoyed every second of Ipswich's run to the final five years earlier when, on an overwhelmingly hot May afternoon at Wembley, we beat Arsenal 1-0 to win the trophy for the first time with our hero on the day, local lad Roger Osborne, so overcome with emotion after he'd scored that he had to be substituted.

Those are the things that dreams are made off. Underdogs against superstars with the Suffolk-born lad who'd been at Ipswich for a decade stealing the headlines away from the footballing royalty that was Liam Brady, Malcolm Macdonald and Alan Hudson – or even, for that matter, our very own England internationals Paul Mariner and my boyhood hero Kevin Beattie.

The biggest day in football had come round again, one that would normally have seen me spend a few hours listening to the radio on that particular afternoon as the scores came through. And, as usual, there were some good games on offer for the neutral, including Chelsea versus Liverpool and Leeds United against Manchester City, while for those who liked a bit of romance in their football, Carlisle United were heading down to Old Trafford to play Manchester United, with my beloved Ipswich due to play at Charlton Athletic.

The only problem was, the biggest day in English football's domestic calendar was all set to clash with the BDO World Darts Championship Final. So I wouldn't be tuning into *Grandstand* on the BBC on this day at least.

Not that being unable to watch the programme was much of an issue as I was, instead, due to be part of it after the BBC had informed me that, providing I'd beaten Jocky in my semifinal, they'd want to show the first three sets of the final on the programme on that Saturday afternoon. There'd then be a 90-minute break before we played the remaining eight sets live on BBC2 all of which meant, of course that, far from watching the sporting headlines come in on that day, I'd be helping to make them instead.

It all started at 6am, my usual time that week to get up. Breakfast at the hotel with Linda and John followed at 7.30am and that was, on this occasion, more fun than usual as both of them are huge Arsenal fans so, given the FA Cup was going to be big news later on that day, I had some fun in reminding them of the day Ipswich had seen off their strongly fancied team back in 1978. Being able to have a laugh with them was, in all honesty, exactly what I needed that morning. I didn't want to be focusing on my match with Eric until I needed to and, as far as I was concerned, I was going to have a smile on my face over breakfast and enjoy the opportunity to talk about something other than darts for a little while.

That year's final was the first that had been split into two sessions which wasn't, as far as I was concerned, a particularly good thing and I was, in truth, trying to work out the best situation for me to be in at the end of that first session. I couldn't help thinking, for a start, that I wasn't playing in just one final but two. So my mindset was very much set on making sure that, at the end of that first final, the one that would be shown on *Grandstand*, I went into the break on the front foot. Doing so with a 3-0 lead over Eric seemed unlikely but I'd have taken 2-1 all day (and night) long if it was offered me. On top of that, I was also aware that, if Eric turned it on and I was 3-0 down myself, then it was going to be a very long break to sit through, one that I'd no doubt be contemplating not only where I'd gone wrong but also what was needed to get back into the match – although the truth of that situation was that if you gave Eric a 3-0 lead, then you were pretty much out of the picture already.

The challenge was going to be how to deal with that unexpected break in proceedings. I'd never played in front of television cameras prior to this event, so it was all very new to me. But, as the BBC would have been paying the BDO what was then a substantial amount of money to televise the tournament, if they wanted a break between sessions then a break was what we would have. Nobody asked the players and our views on the matter wouldn't have been listened to anyway. But look. In any sport, and at any level, a break in proceedings, whether planned or not, can have a dramatic effect on the course of a match, and not always in a good way. If you're watching a game of football on TV and a team scored a minute or so before half-time, a planned interval, then the commentator will almost certainly say how it's 'always a good time to score before the break'. Now, he or she is right to say that. But they're usually thinking about the team who scored the goal and how it will send them into that break full of confidence and with their tails very much up.

But it's not always as simple as that. Conceding a goal at such a critical time could also be exactly what the other team needed. It's a shock to their system, a dent in their best-laid plans. Their manager will probably give them the proverbial bollocking at half-time and they might come out for the second half full of fire and passion and take the game to the opposition who might, on the contrary, be a little bit complacent at that stage.

So conceding a goal just before half-time may well work to that team's advantage more than it does for the team who scored. And this doesn't just apply in football. Let's look at tennis as another example. In their Wimbledon semi-final in 2001, Tim Henman looked as if he was set to beat Goran Ivanišević when the players were forced to take more than one break because of rain. How would their mindsets have been at that time? I can't say for certain, of course. But I'd feel pretty safe in saying that Ivanišević saw those breaks as an opportunity to refocus on what he needed to do, an opportunity to return to the court and take the game back to Henman, who'd had his rhythm interrupted at the worst possible moment and couldn't pick it up again. Ivanišević won and went on to take the title. Yet if it hadn't rained on those two days, it's almost certain that Henman would have reached the final.

You have to go into a break with your mind in the right place. If you don't, then you are going to be in trouble when things resume. Which is why, with that pending break coming in our match, I focused on being exactly where I wanted to be at that stage, I saw it, felt it in my own mind and knew, as a result, exactly how I'd treat that break. A bit of practice, a bit of chilling out. Nothing too serious but enough to mean I'd be more than ready for Eric when we restarted, 2-1 up or even 3-0 up.

Not too much pressure in either scenario. But 2-1 down? Okay, a little bit of pressure would be on then, but it wasn't a situation that would have been new to me and I'd have coped with it. What I didn't want to be was 3-0 down and I remain convinced, to this day, that I'd got myself into such a good place mentally, that Eric was never going to take a 3-0 lead against me, it simply wasn't going to happen.

It also helped, of course, that the FA Cup third round was being played that day. So I was thinking of how I'd go into the break and look at all of the final scores, including Ipswich's. The fact they were playing had pretty much been on my mind from the moment I woke up to be honest and the opportunity to talk about the football on what was otherwise the biggest day of my life was just right for me as it took my mind off all the match permutations and possibilities that I would, otherwise, have been obsessing about. So, with breakfast (plus a confidently given prediction that Ipswich would see off Charlton later that day) out of the way and with my mind and body in a good place, I headed off to the venue to practise hoping, in the process, to win my first little battle over Eric on the day.

There were two practice rooms at Jollees, one that had two boards in it plus a smaller one called the band room that had just the one. That smaller practice room was, I knew, the one that Eric preferred to use himself so, having arrived three hours before the start of our match, I headed straight in there and started practising. Eric arrived half an hour later and I soon heard that he wasn't happy about having to do his practice session in the bigger room. I also knew he'd wanted me to beat Jocky in the semi-final as he, naturally, felt he had a much bigger chance of beating me in the final than he would have done Jocky, so he now had the pressure of being the overwhelming favourite to win, much as Arsenal had been when they lined up against Ipswich a few years earlier at a sunny Wembley.

A journalist came up to me in 'my' practice room and, given the fact that Eric was now odds-on favourite to win, pointed out to me that I now had nothing to lose to which I could only reply by saying, 'I do, I've a world final to lose.'

I wasn't there to enjoy myself or make the most of the occasion. I wanted to win. People talk in sport now about marginal gains, all the little things you can do that, in isolation, might seem quite insignificant but are, when you amass them all together, examples of the sort of attention to detail that, if things are very tight and could swing either way, might just give you the tiniest of advantages. I hadn't made sure I ended up practising in that smaller practice room before the final by accident, I'd worked out that anything at all that might just have knocked Eric out of his rhythm a little bit could end up making a difference so getting there early enough to get to use it had been part of my plan. The fact that Eric had arrived only half an hour after I'd arrived meant, to me, he'd wanted that room as much as I did and had thought he was in plenty of time to do so. It might all have seemed a case of minor details to most people, even today, but I was confident that it would have given me a little boost at his expense in the build-up.

The first part of the final was due to start at 2.30pm, half an hour or so before Ipswich were due to kick off in their FA Cup match against Charlton, but, prepared as ever, I made sure enough people were aware of the match and my need to know what the score was – at the right moment that is. I didn't think anyone would be daft enough to shout out something along the lines of, 'Keith, Ipswich have just gone a goal down,' just as I was looking to hit double top to win a leg, but you never know what's going to happen with a darts audience, they can be a lively lot. Mind you, I'd probably have hit that double top blindfolded if we'd gone one up but, even so, and as much as I loved my football, all of that had to wait.

I'd never felt an atmosphere quite like the one that greeted Eric and I as we walked on to the stage to begin the match. It was as intense as it gets, an air of expectancy that felt as if it could be bottled. Whether that expectancy was all about Eric winning with ease or the 'kid from Suffolk' pulling off another shock I'm not too sure, a bit of both perhaps although, to be fair, I think most of the people there expected Eric to win.

Just before we'd gone on the stage, I'd said to John and Linda that I needed to win at least one of these three opening sets that were being played on *Grandstand*. I certainly didn't like to think about coming out to finish the match and already being

3-0 down to Eric, who wasn't the sort of opponent who would throw a lead like that away.

Game on then.

The first set is, for me, as important as any you'll play in a match. It's the one where any nerves might still be showing; likewise, if you're going to throw some bad darts, it's probably going to happen at this stage before you and your opponent get into your rhythm. It's the same with most sports. Take the opening five minutes or so in a football match for example. If there's an early goal, it's usually because someone, somewhere has made a mistake. Nerves can show at all levels; in tennis, the elite players can take a while to settle down into a match and if too many errors creep into their game, it's a long road back. Rafael Nadal lost the first set of the 2006 Wimbledon final 6-0, which is a margin you don't want to lose by if you're knocking the ball about on the public courts with a mate, let alone one when you're one of the best players of all time. Losing that first set by such a huge margin would have played on Nadal's mind in the same way I am sure Jocky might have been distracted in our semi-final when he missed that last dart that would otherwise have won him £52,000 – although he certainly didn't show it.

So whatever happened in our first set that day, I didn't want it to be marked by my missing crucial shots. Even if Eric won it, as long as I'd played well, I'd have been confident about getting my act together in the next set, I'd have been into my game and ready to give it a go.

As things turned out, I was hitting the scores I needed straight away and checked out on the bull for a 124 finish to win it 3-1. Which meant that absolute minimum I'd told Linda and John about pre-match, taking at least one of the afternoon sets, had been achieved already. That meant the mental pressure was off me straight away and, if the two we still had to play weren't exactly 'free hits', my confidence had grown and I went into the second set in a far better frame of mind than I had the first. It showed. I needed 47 to win the set and took that out in two darts to win 3-1 again, knowing that, whatever happened now, I'd leave this stage of the final in the lead and, in the process, have some of *Grandstand*'s viewers on the edge of their seats and looking forward to seeing if I could do it all over again in the evening session.

Eric won the third set, 3-1, but, strangely enough this didn't worry me too much. I'd had a good start but not the perfect one as I was worried that, if I did leave the first session 3-0 up then I might have felt a little bit complacent going into the evening session. Not, I should add, intentionally, especially when I was up against an opponent as good as Eric, but, deep down, in situations like that, there is always room in the back of your mind for you to be thinking 'it's all over, I've won this' – that's only natural.

Even if Eric had then pulled a couple of sets back to make it 3-2, off your mind pops again, 'I'm still 3-2 up' – and that's when the complacency can start to get a bit dangerous. So, for me, 2-1 up was perfect; I was ahead but there was still a lot of darts to play and I'd have to be as focused as I'd ever been to see the match out. I got off the stage as quickly as I could and made straight for the practice room. We had a 90-minute break so time for some more practice but, more importantly than that, I wanted to see how Ipswich had got on – and there was more good news, they'd beaten Charlton 3-2 after going 2-0 down while I'd been playing. I'm sure everyone heard the big cheer that came from my practice room and wondered what on earth Keith Deller was getting so excited about – perhaps they thought I'd already thought I'd won. Which, despite my lead, was anything but the case.

* * *

Ipswich's win did help to put me in a relaxed frame of mind over the break period, and I was happy to use it keeping my practice up and doing nothing too intense or serious other than focusing on staying in the rhythm I was in when we returned to the stage. I've always been serious about practising; folk can say whatever they like about darts and the people who play but it is as important for the men and women who are regularly competing at the very top to practise as it is for any other sporting professional to do so. I got into the habit of regularly practising early on in my career – even when I used to stay at Linda and John's house in Enfield, I'd be at the board with Linda, who was playing for the English ladies' team at the time. I'd play for hour after hour at their place, so much so in fact that I wore out the carpet where the dartboard was.

In the build-up to all the World Championships I played in, I'd regularly practise at The Rising Sun pub in Whetstone and became so much of a regular there that the gentleman who used to look after the referee and officials for Arsenal FC at Highbury back in the day remembers me well, as it was his local. I'd play 501 most of the time as this gave me a bit of competition against whoever I was playing as well as keeping my game sharp, although, whenever I was at Linda and John's, I'd also practise my doubles. Eventually, in 1987, and when I'd moved back to Suffolk, I started to put in a very strict routine for five days a week which would start by taking the kids to school. As soon as I got home again, and this would be at about 9am, I'd loosen up for half an hour or so before playing some 501 games for another 90 minutes or so. I'd then practise my finishes, starting at 80 then, once I'd checked out on 80, I'd move on to 81, then to 82 and so on and so forth, doing this for about an hour and seeing how far I could get in a session that would normally take me up to around noon.

Moving ahead briefly and while I remember, that move back to Suffolk hadn't been intended or even planned. It was more something that was forced, through necessity, on to Kim and myself. I had, by 1987, found myself in a little bit of financial trouble, an ongoing and ever-increasing worry that had built up even though we were both earning decent money at that time. Having said that, it wasn't anything like the income I'd been on in 1983 and in the years beyond that. My mortgage was £500 a month for a start. I was also putting £500 a month into a pension.

And no, that isn't a typo. I really was, back in the 1980s and in my mid-20s, paying that much into a private pension which, without going into too much detail, was a case of someone who knew exactly what he was doing, selling a totally unsuitable and unsustainable financial product to someone who didn't really know very much about pensions and who certainly wasn't, at that time, thinking about retirement. It had been a case of 'where do I sign?' and move on to the next thing. And now, four years after my World Championship win, I was starting to get into serious debt, £11,000 at its peak to be exact. That meant the pressure on me to win games for the money was becoming overwhelming, so much so that I'd tighten up when it came to the important doubles and end up losing the match. This had been building up for a while, and Kim's parents knew full well how worried we were and would help out as much as they could, including taking us out for meals. That was hard for me to take and I was feeling as if I was letting people down but Alec, Kim's dad, always used to say to me that we were young and had to focus on enjoying our lives rather than forever worrying about chasing the money.

In the end, Kim and I decided to put our house up for sale. We didn't want to. We loved the house and had anticipated always living there. But this was a case of 'needs must'. At first we wondered if we'd ever sell it though. The people who viewed it would, more or less, sing its praises – that is, until they saw our swimming pool. Then their expressions changed. They'd claim that their children would fall in the pool, or that their pets would. And that was that. But, eventually, it sold and at a profit as well. We duly moved back up to Suffolk and to the house where we both live today. And, looking back, it was the best thing that could have happened to us. With the burden of debt well and truly lifted from my shoulders, I was able to focus on my darts again.

* * *

Back to that practice routine, the one I was strictly adhering to at the time of my first World Championship. I was focused, but not so much that I would practise all day and, no matter what else was happening, I'd always find the time to have a break for lunch when, more often than not, Kim and I would either go for a walk with our German Shepherd or have a nice pub lunch somewhere – and no, I wasn't tempted to combine that with a quick game against one of the locals. I don't believe in mixing business with pleasure and this was mine and Kim's time.

Following lunch, however, it would be back to practising and I'd play some more 501 games for an hour or so before heading off out again to pick up the kids from school. I'd then end my working day practising again for an hour or so in the evenings, usually on doubles. It probably looks very regimented and, to a certain extent, it had to be. Practice is a discipline; there will be days when you don't want to practise your craft, no matter what it is, and there were days when it was the last thing I wanted to do. Besides, practising at home was much better for me than doing so at my local as, although there'd be no shortage of offers from people to give me a game, most of them couldn't play it and that was of no use to me whatsoever. Exhibitions, on the other hand, were different as, whatever pub or club I happened to be appearing at, I knew that they'd be lining up their best players to give me a game. That was always useful and a good alternative to practising at home as the locals would be hyped up at the prospect of taking on and possibly beating a world champion, so I'd be sure of a few tight games on those nights.

As far as practising at the Worlds was concerned, I still had that routine as well as a preferred place to practise – which, at Jollees, was that smaller room that Eric also preferred to warm up in. These sessions wouldn't be too intense though; the priority was just ensuring I kept my focus and rhythm going between matches. I didn't want my mind to drift off on to anything else, least of all the football. That could wait. I knew that, prior to the second session of the final starting, Eric was going to come at me from the beginning; he'd be going for big scores, the 180s, straight away and putting me under pressure. I was on my own until Terry O'Dea came into the practice room and asked me how I was feeling. He was the first person to do so at that stage. I told him that, whatever happened, Eric wasn't going to get to four sets, so I must have been feeling confident by then. I wasn't over-confident, though, and I would have spent the whole of that break practising was it not for the fact that the BBC wanted to film Eric and me walking to the stage together for the start of the final session, which meant he had to come into my practice room to do so ten minutes beforehand. That wasn't, I think, ideal for either of us.

As I'd always feared, Eric was on fire from the start of the fourth set, hitting a 180 as well as checking out on 140. It was as comprehensive a defeat as I'd had in any of the sets that week but it was also a wake-up call and, in the following set, I hit 180 in three consecutive legs to take it 3-2, meaning I was now leading the match 3-1.

Remember what I said earlier about getting your bad darts out of the way early on? I'd started well and that hadn't happened, but I didn't play at all well in the fifth set and lost it 3-1, then the sixth was even worse. I had some bounce-outs while Eric had a very purposeful look about him as he walked from the board after every throw. He was in the zone and, I am sure, feeling he was now doing enough to win.

That meant, at 3-3, the seventh set was not only going to be the most important one of the match for me but also the week and, quite possibly, my career so far. I knew I had to get back in front to prevent Eric from getting the upper hand as if he won it, it'd be the first time he'd been ahead in the final. The first two legs were close so it was 1-1 when, in the third leg, I needed a 156 checkout which I made, something that gave me an enormous boost and maybe, at the same time, knocked Eric's confidence just a little bit.

With me going 4-3 up, just when he needed to up his game in the same way I had at the beginning of the previous set, Eric started the eighth set by missing a few doubles which let me in to win it 3-2 meaning that, at 5-3 up, I was now just one set away from fulfilling the dream I'd had ever since I first started playing darts and becoming world champion – as well as, of course, winning that bet for Peter Purves.

What a situation to be in. It wasn't one that anyone suspected would ever come to pass when Mum and Dad put that dartboard up in our kitchen – leading 5-3 in the world final and playing against one of the best competitors our game has ever seen. It couldn't get any better than this. Except, of course, it could. I didn't want to be in this situation and then lose the match, I had to make sure I won now. My first chance came in the ninth set, at two legs all and I had a big enough chance for me to think, prematurely, that I was the world champion. But no, I panicked and Eric took full advantage, laughing as he did so. He must have thought, at that stage, that my game had 'gone' and he was probably even more convinced of that after he won the tenth set 3-0. My head was in the shed and I knew I had to refocus immediately, which was easier said than done in that sort of atmosphere. The final was providing some great drama for everyone present, even if, for me, it was the sort of drama that I could do without. The score was now 5-5 which meant we were about to play the darts equivalent of a sudden-death penalty shoot-out – one set to go and winner takes all.

I didn't want to come all this way just to throw it away now.

Eric took the first leg. I'd had a chance to check out on 61 but threw 57, leaving double two. Eric needed double 18 to win the leg and he took it, so for the first time in the match he was ahead.

I checked out with a 12-darter to win the second leg, winning it on double eight. Eric had strayed into the five a couple of times during that leg, scoring a 55 and 30 while I'd thrown 100, 140 and then 140 before checking out on 121.

In the third leg and still needing 418, Eric had a bounce-out with his last dart and scored only 40. That left me with 221 which went down to 126 after I'd scored 95. Eric was still on 378 so the leg was mine to lose and, after he threw 85, scoring a five again in the process, I threw 58, leaving me with 68 to win and to go 2-1 up, which I did with 20, 16 and double 16.

Going into the fourth leg, I knew that if I could win it, I would be the world champion. I needed a couple of seconds to gather my thoughts so had a quick sip of lager beforehand, which did the trick. That was just as well as it was a high-scoring leg from the off with, after nine darts, Eric sat on 121. If he checked out on that then he'd bring the score back to 2-2 with me sat on 138, which wasn't, and isn't, the easiest score to check out on – and Eric knew it, choosing to play the percentage game and scoring 89, even though he could have checked out with the bull. He reckoned, as Sid Waddell confirmed, 'He's banking on Deller not doing it.'

Just 138 to become world champion, then.

Treble 20. Then a treble 18. Is Eric regretting playing that percentage shot now?

'The shot's on for the title … double 12 for the title.'

Double 12. I hit it and do my best Paul Mariner celebration in response as a shocked Sid finds the words he needs to describe what's just happened which is, of course, what absolutely no one except for me expected to see at the climax of this particular tournament.

'I'm telling you, I'm telling you. I've seen nothing like it. Keith Deller of Ipswich, 23 years old. He had to qualify to get here! Bristow did a percentage shot, Deller did the business. He's now the world champion.'

Just as I said I would be.

My life changed with that last throw, immediately and irrevocably. I was now a world champion and, no matter what happened to me in my life from that moment on, that was something nobody could ever take away from me. I walked off the stage in a bit of a daze, shaking a few hands and accepting, gratefully, all the congratulations that were coming my way until I found myself with Linda, who had the biggest smile on her face. She looked as happy as I did as she gave me a big hug, looking much more in control of things and her emotions than me as I continued to walk around that tiny backstage area. More handshakes, more congratulations and, for me, the steady realisation of what I had just achieved beginning to sink in. I was the first player to beat the top three seeds in the world en route to winning the trophy, while the final remains the only one to be split into two segments.

There was no messing about with the presentation, which couldn't start until Eric had resurfaced from the crowd. He'd gone for a quick stroll after I won but was soon back on the stage, the familiar grin showing on his face as he accepted his runners-up cheque and gave everyone a quick wave before, still smiling, disappearing into the crowd again. Then it was my turn and a chance to hold that wonderful trophy aloft to a crowd that had been nothing but raucous throughout but did, at least, give me a few seconds to say a few words which I did, thanking the BDO for introducing qualifiers for that year's championships because, as I commented, if they hadn't made that decision then I wouldn't have had the opportunity to compete that week.

I bet Peter Purves was glad that I did.

The Observer later called it one of the ten biggest upsets in sporting history – ranking my achievement on the same level as the great cricketer Don Bradman being bowled for a duck in his final Test innings, boxing legend Mike Tyson losing to rank outsider James 'Buster' Douglas in their 1990 world heavyweight championship clash (a 'mismatch' according to some), and, here's a footballing one, Hereford United beating Newcastle United in the FA Cup third round in 1972. I've also since learned that Raymond van Barneveld has said watching our final is what made him want to become a professional darts player, while Gary Anderson was quoted in an interview as saying it was the match that made him sit up and 'take notice of darts'.

Even Kim remembers it. She's told me that she came in late on that Saturday night but made sure to ask her parents, 'Did that good-looking younger player win the darts final?'

'Yes, he did,' they told her, adding, 'and it was a great final.' Who would have thought that four decades on we would be celebrating our 36th wedding anniversary!

I'd like to say I partied all night. Endless bottles of champagne and pretty girls on each arm. But there wasn't any chance of that happening as I was absolutely exhausted, so much so that I ended up in my hotel room watching *Match of the Day* with a glass of orange juice and lemonade by my side. I had, to be fair, been invited to the VIP section of one of the local nightclubs but that was never going to happen unless they wanted their newest VIP guest to be seen nodding off in a corner somewhere.

I headed back to Ipswich the following day so I could have some time with my family and friends, as well as have a bit of a private celebration with them. Well, and a few others too, as when I turned up on my street there were about 400 people there ready to greet me as well as some TV people and even some bunting that had been put up, none of which I was expecting. So it was a very special moment for me as I am, and remain, very proud of my upbringing, being brought up on that street by Mum and Dad in a humble council house and learning my trade on the cheap dartboard they decided to buy and put up in the kitchen so they could practice before their games in the local pubs and clubs league.

* * *

Now I was world champion and, even though I'd moved to Enfield, complete strangers would knock on my parents' door and ask them if I lived there. Mum would say yes, and invite them in for a cup of tea before putting the video of my final win on for them. I said to her on more than one occasion that she shouldn't have been letting strangers into their house but she was so proud of me, she just couldn't help herself. All because of that dartboard they put up in the kitchen. Mum and Dad probably hadn't expected me to end up playing on it more than they did between them. So, as household investments go, that dartboard had turned out to be a rather good one.

5

In the Spotlight

My brief was to travel down to the west country
to have a game of darts against a budgerigar.

WHILE IT was good to get back home and spend some time
with Mum and Dad, I knew that I wasn't going to be able to
pop down the pub for a quick pint and game of darts with
them anymore – not unless I wanted everyone in the bar to
immediately challenge me. So much for a quiet night out. It
didn't look as if I'd be having too many of those for a little while.

My life had changed the moment I checked out against Eric
with that double 12. I knew, for a start, that even if I might not
exactly have become a millionaire overnight, I would, providing
I was careful with my money and newly acquired earning power,
never have to worry about paying the bills again, while the
cheque for £8,000 that I'd won, along with the title and trophy,
would more than come in handy. I was never going to be flash
like Bobby George; he's got it off to a fine art and I respect him

so much for not only his skills as a darts player but also how he has cultivated an image for himself which, nearly two decades after he last played in the BDO World Championship, means he is still in demand and will never have to look for work.

What I did find, early on after my win, was that the demands on my time suddenly went through the roof. Everyone suddenly wanted to have a bit of me and, although it was fun at first, it also meant I found I wasn't having as much time to practise as I would have liked.

Things were especially hectic in the days after my title win. I was invited to appear on the BBC's *Breakfast Time* television programme, being interviewed by Selina Scott, as well as appearing on a load of other shows – so many now that, I confess, I can't remember them all. There was one that I will never forget though and that was my appearance on the popular US drama series *Hart to Hart*, which starred Robert Wagner and Stefanie Powers as a wealthy couple who kept on finding themselves doing a little bit of unofficial detective work on the side – and invariably solving the case. The show was very popular here, so they filmed two episodes in England which focused on their gardener who ended up becoming a murderer – he also, by coincidence, happened to be the captain of his local pubs darts team, which was where I came in, throwing some darts while at the same time wearing Robert Wagner's rings, which were so heavy that I couldn't throw properly! I thought he might have let me keep them but, sadly, he wanted them back again.

I also did *A Question Of Sport* a couple of times, which was a lot of fun. It had always been one of my favourite shows, so to find myself as part of one of the teams was great. I had to put a great deal of thought into my wardrobe, mind you, as I could hardly sit there with my darts gear on – which was all that most people would have ever seen me in – so, in the end, I wore a jumper and shirt from Gabicci. The brand has long been championed by the professional golfer Vijay Singh, so at the time of my appearance I reckoned I was in good company. Another famous wearer, however, was Derek 'Del Boy' Trotter in *Only Fools and Horses*. Having said that, my dad and father-in-law are also big fans of the brand so they'd look forward to my yearly visits to the factory where I'd be able to pick out anything I wanted, ending up with, I think, about 40 different jumpers and shirts, which was great.

* * *

I particularly enjoyed the opportunity to meet other sportsmen and women whenever I appeared on *A Question Of Sport*. When I was on the programme shortly after I won the Worlds in 1983, I was part of Willie Carson's team, along with the speedway rider Michael Lee who'd made his name (as well as winning a world title himself) up in King's Lynn in 1980. I appeared on the show again in 1987, on Emlyn Hughes's team, alongside the golfer Ian Woosnam, and, although I can't remember now who was on the opposing side in 1983, I remember who we were up against the second time around – Bill Beaumont, the former England rugby union captain, cricketer Mike Gatting and the Coventry City goalkeeper Steve Ogrizovic. As is often the case with these programmes, they record more than one on the day and I have very fond memories of Frank Bruno being on another edition then. Frank was one of the most famous and recognisable sports stars in the country at the time, and arrived at the studio along with Brian McClair, the Manchester United and Scotland footballer. Kim told me that she'd never heard of Brian though and had initially thought he was Frank's driver, so I just told her he played for Manchester United!

I was also asked to appear on *That's Life*, a light-hearted consumer programme on the BBC that was presented by Esther Rantzen. But they didn't want me in the studio for an interview or anything like that. No, that would have been far too straightforward for Esther. My brief was to travel down to the west country to have a game of darts against a budgerigar. But that wasn't the end of it as they'd also got Sid Waddell in on the act and he came along to commentate, allowing for the very obvious fact that a budgie isn't going to be able to throw a dart, with the dartboard on the ground and the bird dropping the darts on to it. You won't be surprised to learn that I lost. Afterwards, the triumphant budgie was put on my shoulder so they could have both of us in the shot but, as I turned to look at it, I got a few sharp pecks in the neck and started to bleed. I suppose all I can say about it was that it was funny at the time.

Another BBC show I found myself appearing on was *Nationwide*, a news magazine programme that featured all of the local BBC regions and followed the main early evening bulletin at 5.45pm. I was on for about ten minutes being asked what my hobbies were. I had a few at that time but they weren't good enough for John Markovic, who told me to say that golf was one, adding, 'It'll be good for your image.' So, of course, I said I liked a game of golf. The next thing I knew was that the 17th hole at St Andrews, one of the most famous holes on one of the most famous courses in the world, had been booked, and I was going to be filmed playing it while on my ten-day tour of Scotland.

Sandy Lyle and co. didn't have too much to worry about. I promptly hit my tee shot straight into the rough while John, who played off a handicap of four, hit his sweet as you like, straight down the fairway. I then played his second shot and, I suspect, did what everyone was hoping would happen, by hitting it straight into the 'wee burn' while he put my ball on to the green. I then took that shot and putted it in for a par, 'beating' John in the process and, competitive golfer that he was, you could see he wasn't happy. I don't know why as he had said all of this would be good for my image. But it was all good fun and, from being a little bit apprehensive about the whole thing, I ended up really enjoying myself. It was good exposure and shown on prime time television, so as far as John was concerned, a case of mission accomplished. Representatives from Slazenger were in attendance and one said to me that if I wore one of the brand's shirts whenever I was on television, I could pick a set of Slazenger clubs out from the pro shop for myself, which I gladly did, realising, as I did so, that this was the sort of thing I would have to expect now that I was a world champion.

* * *

I even ended up doing a fashion shoot. Magazine editors portrayed me as presenting darts in a whole new way. It had always been seen as the game that was played by overweight men in the back of a smoky bar, who'd have their darts in one hand and pint pot in the other while their kids were marooned outside in the back of a Ford Cortina with a bottle of Vimto and packet of crisps to keep them company. That was, and remains, a terribly exaggerated image of darts and its players, of course, but it prevailed for much of the 1970s and early 80s and, to be fair, the lifestyle of some of the more famous players didn't exactly lend them to being poster boys of any kind. Jocky Wilson always seemed to have a fag in his hand for example, while Leighton Rees admitted, 'When I started out in my younger days, you played darts in a pub and you drank and you smoked. That was the way it was.' I was seen as the man who was changing all of that. I was young, slim, fit and, as far as the watching world was concerned, clean-living. I also preferred a glass of Coke to a beer. So this all went down well with journalists looking for a new angle. I was the proverbial 'new kid on the block' and they made the most of it. One of the shoots I did was at the Stringfellows nightclub, which was a bit strange as it's not normally the sort of place I would have gone to!

But it wasn't all good. The one sure thing anyone can say about getting to the top of their profession, whatever it is, is that as soon as you get there people will want to bring you down again. So I had to be careful with what I ended up doing or even said, in case it came back to haunt me later on. It wasn't, admittedly, quite such an issue back in the 1980s as it is now, what with everyone having a camera on their phones and being on social media, but the potential to get yourself into a spot of trouble was always there. I remember playing my county darts for London at around that time, when we were up against Glamorgan, and in one game that Eric Bristow played in a few of the opposing fans made their way up on to the stage and gave Eric some abuse. It made the sports pages and, in the aftermath, *The Sun* called me and asked for a comment. I didn't really want to say too much, so just said it was a shame that a few people had given Eric some stick on the night, as it had spoilt the event for everyone else.

I thought nothing more of it and, the following week, I was up in Cardiff to play for England in a game against Wales. It was the first time I'd played for my country, so it was a big moment for me. The day before the match, *The Sun* wrote about what I'd said – a few days earlier, that perfectly innocuous statement, paraphrasing my words in a headline that read 'Deller Slams Drunken Welsh Yobs'. Which was just what I needed the day before I was due to play for England in Cardiff. Sure enough, I ended up being booed by 2,500 Welsh darts fans during the match. It didn't end there though. Two hours after it had finished, I was still stuck at the venue. Everyone else had gone home but outside there were around 200 of them ready, waiting and willing to lynch me as soon as I left, so I had to call the police in the end so I could get a safe escort out of the place. At least I'd won my match, but it was a horrible experience all round and not one I'd ever care to repeat.

After that match had been played, all of the top players got together for the Double Diamond Masters tournament, which was big enough to have its final shown on ITV. It was initially played in different regions throughout the country, whittling down the players in each until there were four left who all met for the final. I was drawn to play Timothy Gould while Eric was up against Mike Gregory who had, by then, started his rise to becoming one of the world's top-ranked players. He was good enough at that stage to beat Eric and reach the final while I beat Timothy. I expect ITV was disappointed not to get a repeat of the BDO final as that might have been a big audience draw. Mike was, however, a good player and as tough an opponent as you could have when the stakes were high, so I was very pleased when I won the final 3-1, and, for those three legs, with 15, 13 and 15 darts thrown. So my game was still good and I'd maintained the rhythm that I'd started to build on in my run-up to the World Championship decider.

* * *

What pleased me more was that I'd won the first big televised event to be shown after the Worlds. It is, I think, hard enough to win any high-ranking tournament, whatever the sport, with a world championship the hardest to win of all – look at how many times England's footballers have struggled to do well in the World Cup, failing even to qualify for the final stages in 1974, 1978 and 1994. The only thing I can think of, as sport in general goes, is going on to prove yourself time and time again after you've won a big title. Is the hunger and desire to do well, to do it all over again, still there, or mentally do you think you have reached your peak and never quite reach those heights again? Look at Ian Baker-Finch, the golfer. He won the Open Championship at Royal Birkdale in 1991, as well as having several other high-placed finishes that year. Yet, in the years that followed, his game went to pieces and he never reached the same heights, or even came close to achieving them, again. I didn't want to be the man who won the World Championship and then faded from view altogether. I wanted to keep on competing at the top level for many years afterwards so, for me, winning the Double Diamond Masters so soon after my world title win was evidence that I'd be more than able to compete in the years to come which, happily, turned out to be exactly what happened.

Winning this tournament also led to me becoming the new face of a bitter that was produced by Ind Coope & Sons, which was based in Romford and included the Double Diamond brand as part of its stable of beers. In exchange for its investment in me I ended up touring the country in order to promote Ind Coope and the product, and ended up taking part in 54 consecutive exhibition matches. It was very hard work and, by the end of the tour, the strain of having to be 'switched on' every night, playing great darts and beating all comers was starting to take its toll. I wasn't going to complain mind you, as Ind Coope was paying me a lot of money to be the figurehead of this particular 'road show'. The exposure and growing fame it was also giving me was, I knew, one of the reasons I'd practised for so long and so hard over the previous years – to get to a place like that, where I was playing darts and being paid a lot of money to do so.

Another deal that came my way at around this time was with Winmau. Once I'd signed up with Winmau, the company's darts, which had my name and picture attached to them, started to appear in all sorts of places, including Argos and Index. Winmau also provided me with a new sponsored Datsun Laurel car so, all in all, I was now really beginning to feel the benefits of my win and the high profile it had given me. I was being presented as the new, young and fit face of darts and, after all the years when the sport had been, rightly or wrongly, associated with beer bellies, cigarettes and dingy bars, I was, as the 'alternative' to that, very much in demand with companies who wanted to align themselves with that image. Winmau was a great company to be associated with and is, for me, the best darts company there is, and I remain, to this day, very proud of our close association.

Because I was so busy over these weeks and months, I probably ended up forgetting what day it was on occasions. But that was the price I had to pay for all the good things that were coming my way. I was earning good money, I can't deny that. But I had to work very hard for it. Long days, long journeys and late nights. Shaking more hands than I'll ever remember and signing autographs by the crate load. I'd become a commercial entity in my own right, the face of Ind Coope and Winmau, along with others. And, I'll stress again that it was, for all the hard work, very enjoyable too. But I was still a professional darts player and I had to find the time and space to prepare for, practise and compete in the big tournaments which, as the popularity of the game continued to spread, were going to come along at regular intervals.

One of them was the British Professional Championship, which was held in Redcar. I arrived there to play my first match following another tiring round of exhibitions and appearances that had taken me anywhere in the world, it seemed, where there was a dartboard. I'd do all the PR stuff on behalf of my sponsors before and after the matches, all of that on top of a three-hour show. All of that came before I had to, hurriedly and with hardly any practice beforehand, take on Gerry Haywood in my first match there.

I was, of course, promoted and introduced as the new and reigning BDO world champion and I'm sure that, especially after my subsequent win in the Double Diamond, big things were expected of Deller yet again but there was no chance of anything like that happening. I was tired and felt pretty much all played out, which meant that Gerry was able to take full advantage and he saw me off, easily, to the tune of a 3-0 scoreline.

Team Unicorn, my first darts team.

Kim and I at home in 1986 along with our beautiful dog, Sheba.

Five up! L-R, Denis Ovens, Dave Lee, me, Billy Dunbar and Clive Pearce (1982)

I had to get used to smiling for the cameras after my world championship win

With the Ipswich Town team following my world championship win — I used to be a ball boy at Portman Road!

Dressed to kill! A photo shoot with Eric Bristow and Jocky Wilson

Warming up for the 1983 British Darts Open.

British Darts Organisation World Final against Eric Bristow in 1983

Eric is having a wardrobe-related issue as John Lowe and I join him on stage

Winning the Double Diamond Masters in 1983, beating Mike Gregory.

Kim and I on our wedding day.

Lauren and Matthew pose for a school photo.

Winning the British Professional Championships in 1987.

A study in concentration at the PDC Skol World Championships in 1999.

Beating Eric was always a good feeling!

With darts legend Tony Green.

Celebrating at the Betfred League of Legends tournament in Stoke-on-Trent.

With Cliff Lazarenko at Kempton Park racecourse.

Eric and I at the William Hill Lincoln Trial Day at Wolverhampton racecourse

With Bobby George (who still refers to me as 'the boy') at a charity fundraiser.

Phil Taylor – the greatest.

The legend that is Eric Bristow

Teaching some of the West Ham lads how to play the game.

Keith Deller

	Sets	
5		5
Eric Bristow		Keith Deller
1	Legs	2
32		**138**

The design for my 2022 competition shirt.

138

Proud parents! Kim and I with our daughter Lauren on her graduation day.

Enjoying a night out at The Dorchester with Kim.

Bobby George and I with aspiring darts star Justin Lee Collins.

With Shaun Wallace from ITV's The Chase – he asked for a photo!

Mike Tindall joins Eric and me – the Tindall's like their darts.

That early exit was just what I needed though as it gave me a chance to slow down a bit, take stock of what I'd achieved so far as well as, importantly, work on what I wanted to achieve in the years and months to come – which was to play in and compete well in as many of the leading ranking tournaments as possible. I'd still have the personal appearances to do as well as all of my sponsor-related commitments but, above all, I needed to compete and I made sure everyone around me was aware of that.

One thing people will often say about darts, especially when they're comparing it to other sports, is that it must be fun to play and with no pressure attached to it whatsoever. If only that was the case. Right from the start of my career, we were all under pressure but not, as you might expect, to win the big titles (or the smaller ones) or, as was increasingly the case, make sure we got the best sponsorship deals.

No, the pressure in darts was all about keeping your world ranking as high as possible. I'd quickly learned that I had to eat and sleep world ranking points because, as a professional, you had to be in the majors regularly in order to get the television exposure that would, in turn, affect your earning power on the exhibition circuit. The more you were on television the greater your negotiating powers were, which meant the higher your ranking was, the more you'd appear in the televised tournaments.

The rankings system worked according to the tournament you were playing in. If it was the World Championship or World Masters, the winner got 12 points towards their total, the runner-up ten, the losing semi-finalists eight, the losing quarter-finalists four and, finally, those who went out in the first round – usually of 32 – would get just two points. Other lower-profile events would also see you earn some ranking points but they wouldn't be so high, so, for example, the winner of the Danish Open would get eight points and the runner-up four.

Believe me, you soon got obsessed with these numbers and what you needed to get, at any given time, to at least maintain your position.

One example I can give about chasing ranking points occurred in the late 1980s when I decided to take part in a tournament in Gosford. Except this wasn't the pleasant town of that name in Oxfordshire but the suburb of Gosford which is about 50 miles north of Sydney in Australia. With those ranking points in mind, my logic in travelling out there was sound enough in what would otherwise have been a long and costly trip. On this occasion, points were up for grabs so, as I was desperate to keep my ranking, I decided that made it worth going. Bob Anderson was travelling out there as well and, in my mind, I thought that the worst I would do is end up as runner-up to Bob as the rest of the field would be Australian players who wouldn't cause me too many problems.

In fact my main worry was the snakes and spiders I knew would be lurking in assorted nooks and crannies out there and, in all likelihood, in my hotel room and just waiting for me to arrive. I'm petrified of both and, just before I left, I wisely (not) did the very best thing I could have done by looking them all up online and finding out just how deadly most of them were. Nice work Keith, I'd be walking on very delicate egg shells as a result.

* * *

Spiders and snakes or not, I wanted those ranking points. So, on the Wednesday of the week before the event started, I headed out of Heathrow, arriving in Sydney the following Friday morning. Once I'd checked into the hotel, I stayed in my room all day to rest up after the long flight, making sure that I tucked all of my bed sheets in as tightly as I could in order to prevent any spiders joining me. I didn't get any sleep at all mind you, as every little noise I heard over the following 12 hours or so was, I convinced myself, a marauding snake or spider with Deller on its mind.

As a result of all that, I ended up at breakfast that Saturday morning feeling like death warmed up anyway – and hadn't seen even the tiniest hint of any of the creepy crawlies I was so worried about. I made my way to the venue, still feeling rough and proceeded to lose in the first round to one of the Australian players I'd expected to beat, then shook hands with him before heading straight back to my hotel, changing my flight time and leaving the next day, arriving back in the UK on the following Monday. Australia and back in five days, out of pocket and no ranking points either.

In 1986, a small group of us headed out to Turku to play in the Finnish Open. Turku was not that far, certainly in terms of possibly being in harm's way from the nuclear accident that had taken place at Chernobyl earlier that year and, as a consequence of that, the BDO had strongly advised its players not to take part in the tournament. The governing body, rather ominously, added that, if any of us did choose to travel out there, we were doing so entirely at our own risk and contrary to the advice we had received.

But there were ranking points up for grabs. And I reckoned that the fall-out from not getting them when they were available was worse than any radioactive fall-out that might be gently drifting earthwards while I was in Turku.

Most of my fellow players took heed of the BDO's advice and chose not to take part. But I was joined by Jocky Wilson, Mike Gregory and Peter Evison in thinking that it was too good an opportunity to turn down, so we all made our way out there. As it turned out, we'd all made the right decision as our little quartet ended up making up the semi-final field, where I lost to Mike, but I wasn't too bothered by that as what really counted was that getting to the last four gave me four precious points to my rankings total.

I was living in Enfield at the time while my in-laws lived at Wood Green, which isn't that far from Heathrow and is on the Piccadilly line on the London Underground. Thus, safely back in the UK from Finland, I arranged to be picked up by Kim at the station. I'd been working out what the new rankings would be, post-Turku, and the four points I'd got out there had put me back in the world's top eight, so I was ecstatic, so much so that, when the train arrived at Wood Green, I leapt off to see Kim, completely forgetting my suitcase, which was now on its way to Cockfosters. I told one of the staff at Wood Green what I'd done, so they had to call Cockfosters in order to tell them they didn't need to worry about the lone piece of luggage now arriving at their station. I ended up getting a (well deserved) telling off from one of the staff members who worked at Wood Green who most emphatically told me what my actions might have caused but, as deeply apologetic and embarrassed as I was, I couldn't help think that it had all been worth it for those four ranking points I'd won.

The World Cup also meted out ranking points but this worked to the disadvantage of the English players as there was a time when five out of the top six in the world were English (the noble exception to that was Jocky Wilson) but, with the World Cup being a four-man event, one of the five – through that format, rather than any fault of his own – would have to miss out. This led to the situation where you could be English and ranked at number six in the world but not be able to go after the big points on offer in the World Cup, while a player from Wales who may have been number seven, eight, nine or even further down could be part of their team, have a great tournament and end up going above you in the rankings.

If you did get picked to play for your country, you got five points automatically. But if you then played badly and got dropped, you might miss out on all the following internationals for a whole year and miss out on a lot of ranking points.

See what I mean about it all getting into my head – I could hardly sleep some nights.

To represent England, you had to play for your county. I remember one time when I had the fifth best county average in the whole of the UK. This should have meant my subsequent selection to play for England was an absolute given, or so you'd have thought. One of the selectors was from my county and I remember saying to him, jokingly, at that time, 'I suppose I'm dropped?' only for him to reply, to my sheer astonishment, that yes, that was the case on this occasion. I couldn't believe it and, during the very heated argument that followed, I pointed out to him exactly where I was in the averages. It didn't make a bit of difference and he didn't even try to explain why the decision had been made. I put it down to jealousy on someone's part. That was it for me and I vowed I'd never play for England again, even if I was picked.

This was picked up by one of the sports journalists in *The Sun*, and the newspaper soon ran a story about it, complete with the headline 'Deller Knifed In The Back'.

Life was hectic. I was either playing darts, thinking about darts or staying awake at night trying to work out all the various permutations of the rankings system. But I did have a rare day off that September. There was not a dartboard to be seen as I went to a wedding and met the woman who would end up being my wife, Kim. It was her brother's wedding, although I didn't sweep her off her feet, at least not on that day as all I can remember is saying 'hello' and thinking how pretty she was. And that was that as, not long after the wedding, I was back on the road. One of the big tournaments that year was the British Matchplay which took place north of the border in Great Yarmouth.

It was being held in Norfolk, the home county of Ipswich Town's biggest rivals, Norwich City. Ipswich and Norwich are the two biggest football clubs in East Anglia and, perhaps surprisingly, as there has never been any antipathy between the two places or counties historically, the rivalry between the two sets of supporters can be a bit lively at times. There wasn't any sign of it at the British Matchplay, which was featured on Anglia TV, as I had some great support there from darts fans from both Suffolk and Norfolk, the sort of loud and vocal backing that can, on occasions, make you feel as if you're already one leg up when you take to the stage. It certainly helped me as I got to the final where, much to the delight, I am sure, of Anglia, I was due to meet Eric in what would have been our first tournament encounter since the BDO final eight months earlier. It was a great match as well, one that people have since called the 'best British Matchplay Final ever' and, even though Eric won 3-2, I was proud to, again, have been part of such a memorable game.

The British Matchplay was a prestigious tournament at the time. It featured the top eight players in the British rankings which meant, as the system worked at the time, you also had the top eight players in the world all at the same venue. Everyone who was there would have fancied their chances of winning and the only real way you might have got some sort of advantage over your opponent – always high quality whoever you were playing – came via the way it was decided who threw first in the match.

Back then, they used a bag which had a green ball and a red ball in it. Each player took a ball and the one who picked out the green ball threw first and therefore had that slight advantage over his opponent. Unfortunately for me, in that deciding leg, Eric drew out the green ball which meant that, even though I had 62 left after 12 darts, after throwing 100, Eric had 32 left to win and hit the double 16 with his first dart before turning to me and, great sportsman that he was, shaking my hand and saying 'great match' before enjoying his win with his fans.

A month later, Eric was my team-mate as we were selected, along with John Lowe and Dave Whitcombe, to represent England in the World Cup, which was being held in Edinburgh. No prizes then, for guessing which team the fervent home support weren't particularly keen on. It was, again, a really good tournament that saw some great matches and darts played, with, at the semi-final stage, Sweden joining the host nation, along with England and Wales. Scotland then went on to beat Sweden 9-1 in the first semi-final while we beat Wales 9-3. That meant the final was going to be the one that everyone wanted and it ended up being one of the most exciting team games I have ever played in.

We were up against a very strong Scotland quartet that consisted of Jocky Wilson, Danny Cunningham, Peter Mason and Harry Patterson, which meant it was never going to be as one-sided as the two semi-finals had been. It was tight enough in fact for the score to be 8-8 when John took to the stage to take on Jocky in the decider. I'd already played Jocky in the singles tournament and at one point had three darts to go 3-0 up against him in a best of seven match. It didn't happen and, with all the support most definitely for Jocky, he went on to win. But, despite all of that loud backing for Jocky and Scotland, John beat him in the decider and I was now a darts world champion in its team event as well as the individual one so, all in all, it hadn't been a bad year at all.

* * *

That November saw me take in the sights and sounds of Muswell Hill one afternoon as I went out with some friends for some much needed downtime. My friend Paul Croft was chatting to a girl called Tracey at a fish and chip shop, mentioning, as he did, that his mate fancied her sister. We've all been there haven't we, that 'my mate fancies your mate' line, beloved of chippies all over the country. Sometimes it works and sometimes it doesn't but, on this occasion, it worked as Tracey's sister was Kim, the girl I'd taken more than a shine to (but didn't do anything about it) at that wedding I'd gone to back in June. I'd remembered Kim but I didn't know if she'd remembered me.

Anyway, one thing led to another as Tracey gave me Kim's number so I gave her a call and we arranged a date which was a meal at a restaurant in Southgate called Corky's. We got on really well and, first date or not, I knew this was the girl I wanted to spend the rest of my life with. For our second date, I went around to her house and met her parents. Kim's dad, Alec, said it was good to meet me, adding, almost as an afterthought, that he 'had two lovely daughters and if anyone laid a hand on them, they wouldn't need a hospital'.

'You won't have any problems with me,' was my reply, and Alec and I went on to have a great relationship.

As 1983 drew to a close, I prepared myself for the last big tournament of the year, the World Masters, over the weekend of 9 and 10 December. I wanted to do well, not only because it would mean I'd ended the year well and would, as a consequence, be on a high prior to the World Championship and having to defend my title a year on from my win at Jollees, but also because the World Masters was a very prestigious tournament that featured 128 players, as well as some hopefuls who'd play in the qualifiers. With its sets being decided by whoever was the first player to win two legs, it also meant that matches could be over quickly and there might always, with it, be a surprise or two. It was the FA Cup of darts, with a lot of matches to be played, in a tournament that was sponsored by Winmau, a company I have always had a good relationship with, so for me there was yet another reason to do well.

I was seeded at six and started well enough on the Saturday, beating Jean-Luc Leclercq 2-0 in the first round before winning 2-1 against Rick Daniels in the second round, or round of 64 as they all now seem to be called at that stage. Next up was Welshman Owen Thomas and another 2-0 win, which meant I was in the last 32 and a fourth-round match against another Englishman, Dave Lee. I knew Dave well as we'd played and practised together many times over the years and he had also been a team-mate of mine when we'd gone over to the USA to play as part of our team in the North American Open.

Dave was a good player but someone I thought I should be beating. But I didn't. Dave was on his game that night and beat me 2-0, before going on to knock out Bob Anderson in the quarter-finals and then losing to Mike Gregory in the semi-finals. It was a good tournament for Dave then but an even better one for Eric, who beat Mike in the final in a result that would have put him in the perfect state of mind for the forthcoming Worlds where he was, by now, the odds-on favourite to win.

It was a disappointing end to what had, for me, been a fantastic year. But, as Christmas, spent with Kim, came and went and the World Championship started to loom very large on the horizon, I found that I didn't have that spark or the confidence that I'd taken up to Stoke-on-Trent a year earlier. Put it this way, if I'd bumped into Peter Purves again, I might not have talked up my chances as much as I had done before. I knew I *could* win it again of course, as I rarely, if ever, entered a big tournament without thinking I could win, but I hadn't been playing well and my early exit at the World Masters had confirmed what I already knew – my game wasn't at the level it needed to be if I was going to retain my title. It was one I'd grown very attached to and had given me the sort of opportunities and profile that no amount of money could ever buy.

Winning a World Championship had been an enormous challenge in itself. But, as any competitor at the top of his or her game will tell you, winning any sport's ultimate prize is difficult enough, but going on to retain it is a lot more difficult as you are now the person or team in everyone else's sights, the one who everyone wants to beat.

I was about to find out how difficult that was going to be.

6

Mr and Mrs Deller

I didn't want to go through all of that again
and, more importantly, I didn't want to put
Kim through it either!

SATURDAY, 31 December 1983. A year since I'd looked Peter Purves in the eye and told him that I'd be the world champion by the end of the week. The words of a confident man.

I arrived for the World Championship as the reigning champion and had been expected to do all of the media duties someone in that position has to do in the days leading up to the tournament with, predictably, the most frequently asked question being, 'Keith, can you win it again?'

It was the sort of pressure I hadn't had to worry about previously. All of the spotlight had been on Eric, John and Jocky. It was the sort of question they were used to answering while I, on the other hand, had arrived quietly and with little ceremony and only had to think about my darts, which suited me fine. This was different as I was now the centre of attention, so much so that, a few days before, I'd been asked by Channel 4's news team to do an interview during which I was told that, if I retained my title during the following week, I'd become the first millionaire darts player.

Whether or not they intended to put any pressure on me with that statement, it worked. I'd come into the tournament on the back of my poor performance in the World Masters and hadn't played well there whereas a year previously, I'd arrived at the Worlds having just breezed my way through qualifying and feeling as if I could beat anyone. Now a part of me was wondering if I'd ever get past the opening match so I kept telling myself, again and again, 'Don't go out in the first round, don't go out in the first round.'

It was like a mantra.

At least the omens were good and that gave me a little bit of hope. I'd been drawn to play against Nicky Virachkul who, of course, I'd played at the same stage the year before. Was history repeating itself? I hoped so. Nicky was the seventh seed when I played him then but was unseeded now, whereas I'd been seeded as six[2]. I might have been higher had it not been for my poor performance at the Masters, where I'd been knocked out by Dave Lee, who'd gone all the way to the semi-finals. Dave's good

---

2   Full seedings for 1984 World Championships: 1 Eric Bristow; 2 Jocky Wilson; 3 Dave Whitcombe; 4 Cliff Lazarenko; 5 John Lowe; 6 Keith Deller; 7 Stefan Lord; 8 Bobby George.

tournament there meant he was now seeded at three, the sort of position I might have expected as a bare minimum, especially as I was coming in as reigning champion. Darts seedings reflect current form, though, so I couldn't argue and knew that Nicky would fancy his chances.

He would have been justified in doing so. Nicky beat me 2-1 and I was out. I didn't want to hang around and was away and gone as soon as I was able to do so, with Linda driving me back to London. It was New Year's Eve and, rather than spending it getting some practice in before an orange juice and early night, Kim and I ended up in Covent Garden where I saw 1984 in by sitting on a step outside a bar with Kim and a bottle of champagne and only able to say one thing to her:

'I'm out of the World Championships.'

A few months later I was back in the company of Eric Bristow, who'd won the Worlds by beating Dave Whitcombe 7-1 in the final, along with John Lowe as we teamed up to represent England in the Nations Cup Triples. Darts-wise it didn't, for me, get much better than having the then number one and two players in the world as your team-mates in any competition, and I knew we'd be hard to beat, especially as Eric was still on a high after winning up in Stoke-on-Trent.

The Nations Cup was a big tournament that was shown on ITV and, given the company I was going to be in, I felt up for it and knew I was going to play well. That was refreshing after how I'd been feeling prior to playing Nicky and it showed as I won all of my matches and we won the tournament into the bargain, something that gave me an enormous boost, reminding me of just how good a player I was, or, maybe, still was. I took that form and confidence with me into that year's British Matchplay where, after beating Eric and John, I made it to the final where my opponent would be Mike Gregory. I came close to winning as well, having about 11 darts to do so, but I ended up getting stuck on double one and Mike took full advantage. It was disappointing to win but at least my game was on the up again; I'd made another final and I should have won. It was the perfect prelude to what I knew would be the biggest challenge of the year for me, the World Masters.

Biggest challenge? I should say so. I was heading into that tournament knowing that I had, as an absolute bare minimum, to make the last 16 or I would fall out of the world's top 16 and, because of that, I'd miss out on the following month's World Championship. Failing to qualify for the Worlds two years after winning it wasn't something I wanted on my CV but that was how it was going to be. Darts rankings are worked out on a one-year cycle so most of our points come from the Worlds and the Masters, which meant that another poor performance would be enough for me to lose that precious place among the world's elite players.

When I arrived at the Rainbow Rooms in Kensington, one of the very first people I bumped into, and quite literally, was the former England and Liverpool football captain Emlyn Hughes. We had a chat and I confessed to him that I needed to play well over the coming few days because, if I didn't, I'd lose that place in the top 16, a bit, I told him, like Liverpool being relegated. Unlikely as that was, for me it would have felt like being relegated to the Second Division. Emlyn took in everything that I'd said and became my unofficial cheerleader at the event, watching all of my matches and giving me all the encouragement that he could – which, for someone as lively as Emlyn, was quite a lot.

It was very welcome.

I beat John Skillet in the first round fairly comfortably, setting up a meeting with Malcolm Davies from Wales. Malcolm wasn't one of the big names at the time but, take it from me, he was an excellent player and I knew it was going to be a very tough match indeed. It was as well. But, feeding off all of the encouragement and positivity that Emlyn had ignited within me (what a character he must have been in the Anfield dressing room, especially if the Reds were losing; he'd have done a fair few captain's talks at such times), I won 2-0 and, from a point where I wasn't even sure I'd get past the first round, I was now positively charged and ready to take on the world, or, at least, my next opponent, who was John-Joe O'Shea from Ireland. Another good win there meant I was now in the last 16 which not only meant, much to my relief, I'd remain in the world's top 16 for 1985 but would also be up front on the stage and playing my remaining matches on television.

It was probably the tie of the round as well as my opponent in the next stage was my friend and old foe John Lowe, who was seeded at two. But, again, I played well and saw John off

2-1, reaching the quarter-finals and a match against Dave Lee. Another win. So I was now, almost unannounced, in the semi-finals and about to play against John Walls, a lad from the north-east, for a place in the final. John had done well to get to this stage of the tournament but the way the draw had worked out meant that I hadn't, until now, met any of the seeds or game's big names. So this would be a tough match for him. He rose to the occasion as well and threw some good darts, but I never felt I was going to lose and played well again, beating him 2-1.

It's funny how things turn out. I'd gone into the tournament worrying about my form and my game in general as well as the very real possibility of making another early exit and dropping out of the top 16. Darts has always had its big-name players. Every decade from the 1970s onwards has seen the most famous players go on to become household names and, in doing so, make a good living out of what had previously been considered a pub game. Yet, for every Eric Bristow, John Lowe and Jocky Wilson, there were dozens and dozens of others, all on the tour and playing in as many tournaments as possible, hoping that they might, one day, become one of the top names themselves. There were, and always will be, a lot of them. And, as is the case in all sports, not everyone can become a star.

I think, deep down, I was worried about slipping down to that level myself. I'd been world champion and had enjoyed a fantastic year as a result of that. Once you've experienced it, all you ever want to do is win more and more titles. It's what drove Sir Alex Ferguson on at Manchester United; the very second he'd guided his team to a trophy, he'd start working on how they were going to win the next one. That was what I wanted for myself and why that World Masters was so important a tournament for me, a defining one almost. I could have gone out early and then struggled to motivate myself to get back up to the top of the game again or I could have played well and, in the process, reminded everyone what I was all about.

Which, I hoped, I'd done. My focus had been on getting to the last 16 yet, here I was in the final, complete with all the ranking points it would have got me and, waiting for me on the stage in that final was Eric, a man who never doubted his ability to win tournaments from one year to another. He was on fire as well, having averaged 101.73 in his semi-final win over Fred McMullan, the highest in the tournament, so I knew it was going to be difficult to beat him while he was in that sort of form. Over a few sets, as in the Worlds, maybe there's always a chance. But the World Masters Final was first to three sets which meant winning the first one was crucial, and Eric did exactly, that by two legs to one. It was, from then on, as tough as it gets in a darts match and, although I stayed with Eric I couldn't quite get ahead and, in the end, he won 3-1.

As if his average score in the semi-final wasn't spectacular enough, Eric nearly matched that against me with 101.16, while mine was 86.55. Eric ended up with four out of the top five averages over the tournament (101.73; 101.16; 93.93 against Ceri Morgan and 93.87 against Steve Brennan), while, in fifth place, with a three-dart of average of 92.55 came yours truly. So I'd done well and, even though I'd lost the final, I considered the tournament a case of 'job done' and felt that, all in all, it had been almost but not quite the perfect end to a year that had, at one point, felt as if it was getting away from me.

Getting to the final also meant I'd be heading off to the World Championship in a far more upbeat frame of mind than I had a year earlier when my confidence had been pretty close to rock bottom and I'd slipped out and away from proceedings after being knocked out in the first round by Nicky Virachkul. Then, much to, I am sure, his astonishment as well as mine, we'd be drawn to play against one another at the first-round stage for the third consecutive year. The score, as far as that personal duel was concerned, was now 1-1, with me having won our match in 1983 followed by Nicky getting his revenge a year later. Things felt different this time around though. I'd gone into that World Championship low on both form and confidence and, after Nicky had beaten me, I couldn't wait to get the hell out of there and back to London where a very maudlin New Year's Eve with Kim had followed. I didn't want to go through all of that again and, more importantly, I didn't want to put Kim through it either.

* * *

It was payback time for Nicky and job done with a fairly straightforward 2-0 win. That set me up for a second-round match with Luc Marreel from Belgium. Luc was a solid player but he'd played in four previous World Championships without getting past the second round and, as far as I was concerned, he wasn't going to do so this year either. He didn't. I had a 91 average and won 3-0. I'd averaged 79 against Nicky, so this was a major step forward in every sense of the word, a high average and no sets lost so far. John Lowe was my opponent in the quarter-final and I should have won. I look back at that match now and the way I'd started, with eight 180s in the first seven legs, meant I was on fire, playing as well as I'd done for years and enjoying every second of what was turning into a wonderful game.

Except when I missed two darts at 52 which would have put me 2-0 up in sets. Twenty, double 16. Missed it. I scored a total of 11 180s in that match and checked out to win one leg on 164 with my average at 100.19, which was the first time a figure of over 100 had been recorded in the World Championship. It really was as good a match as I've ever played in. I felt that I was going to get whatever score I wanted every time I visited the board. But that missed 52 cost me very dearly. I'm convinced, to this day, that if I'd beaten John then I'd have made the final again. I'd have been up against Cliff Lazarenko in the semi-final and would have more than fancied my chances of beating Cliff at that stage. Then it would have been Eric again. It's all in glorious hindsight now of course, but that missed 52 is, for me, what cost me a second World Championship. A tiny, tiny margin but one that made all the difference that year. I could go back there again today and hit that 52 19 times out of 20 with no problems at all.

Eric went on to beat John in the final to firmly establish himself as the number one player in the world. And that was well deserved. But my defeat to John dropped me down to number seven in the rankings and I knew from then on in that I'd be spending the rest of that year looking to get myself back up into the world's elite, and staying there. So there was a lot to play for and, at still just 25 years old (two years younger than Eric and 14 years younger than John), I was looking forward to the challenge and proving, in the process, that I was still one of the best players around.

The highlight of the year had nothing to do with darts, however. Kim and I got married on 22 June in Enfield. Mind you, Ipswich was well represented on the day as I'd arranged for a coach to travel down with all of my family and friends on board so we all ended up having a wonderful day surrounded by our very nearest and dearest – and not a dartboard in sight! In the evening, a photographer from the local Enfield newspaper took our photograph, which ended up on the front cover the next day – the very first time the paper had ever printed a colour cover, so it was nice to be part of a bit of local press history. We then headed off to the New Forest for our honeymoon, a modest affair perhaps but that was because we would both be going to Las Vegas two months later where I'd be playing in the North American Open, a world ranking event, so it was important for me to be there and competing, and an ideal opportunity for Kim to come along as we could, between the matches, see a few shows. We loved going there anyway and it was extra special this time around as so many people kept coming up to us to offer their congratulations, so it was a great trip all round.

I felt very lucky as Kim's family were all lovely people. Her brothers, John and Paul, would regularly come and watch me play at BDO events as Sally, who was John's wife, was the niece to Olly Croft, then the chairman of the BDO. Kim also has a sister, Tracey, who is married to Steve. They have two grown-up children, Alex and Kate, and we all meet up regularly to go out for a meal and to just enjoy each other's company. Kim also has a wonderful great aunt and uncle in Laurie and Lilly, who are lovely people we'd regularly go to visit, along with our dog Sheba. Laurie was a tools man by trade and he'd put new dart points in for me whenever I needed them. In addition to that, Mum and Dad took to Kim straight away and loved her like the daughter they'd never had. They'd seen, over time, how good for me she was and were as proud as anyone on our wedding day, able to say that they were now her parents as well. Both sets of parents gave us so much from the beginning; they understood the demands of my career and all the travelling that went with it and even made it possible for Kim to accompany me by taking over 'parenting' duties whenever required.

This was just as well, because Kim travelled around the world with me almost straight away. I didn't see the need for – and neither did I want – her to stay at home while I was away, so we ended up heading out to all my exhibitions as well as all the tournaments I competed in as the proverbial happy couple, one of which had been the 1984 Jersey Open where we got engaged.

Most of the other players didn't, for varying reasons, take their wives with them while they were working, but my attitude was that it would be good if we could see as much as we could of the world together and with little to no responsibilities before we started a family, as it wouldn't be so straightforward then. One early event that we both really enjoyed was held in Japan where the hotel we were staying at was situated opposite Disneyland in Tokyo, so we ended up having a great view of the firework display every night.

We particularly enjoyed heading out to Canada for tournaments, so much so that, one year, I made sure that once my commitments in those were done and dusted, I followed up with a ten-day exhibition tour that took us right across the country. We'd always find the time to explore and do whatever was popular with tourists wherever we were. On one occasion we were looking to go horse riding (great for Kim, who loves horses but not much fun for me as they make me nervous) when, in the middle of a two-hour trek in the back of beyond, we came across a sign that you didn't tend to see in the Suffolk countryside, reading 'BEWARE OF BEARS'.

It quickened my pulse, put it that way.

I looked for the guide and, trying to look as if I wasn't really worried at all (I was), said to him, 'What happens if a bear comes up close to us?'

'Can you ride, Keith?'

'No.'

'You'd better learn quickly then.'

I had an exhibition that same night. Yet, despite the nerves that seeing the sign had given me, I ended up playing really well and even broke the record there for the number of 180s scored, so maybe they should release a few bears into the Suffolk countryside.

I love visiting Canada and have many great memories of trips taken over there. In 1995, I was captain of an eight-man team that had been put together to take on the host nation at a venue in Calgary – one of the places, I should add, where there are more than a few bears around. There would be no treks or horse riding this time however, just a chance for my team, which also featured Phil Taylor and Rod Harrington, to take on the locals. I'm sure the other lads were more than happy to come with me, although it might have helped them to make up their minds when I told them we'd be heading out there via Air Canada in business class. It was a great trip, made even more enjoyable for me as I was able to play in the doubles with Phil, a man who has taken darts to another level and is, in my opinion, the greatest player the game has ever seen.

I also enjoyed the promotions we did at race meetings. I went to Newmarket races one day, along with Eric Bristow and Russ Bray, the referee and caller. We were usually there for the prestigious Guineas Festival, which was held over two consecutive days, and the place was absolutely packed out. An event in 2007 particularly springs to mind. We had the darts exhibition in a big marquee that was near the parade ring and the excitement was growing as the big race of the meeting, the

2000 Guineas Stakes, was about to start. One of the horses running in it was called Cockney Rebel, which just happened to be Eric's nickname. So, because of that, everyone was lumping money on it but, unlike Kim and my son Matthew, I was playing safe and betting on the favourite, telling anyone who'd listen that a horse priced at 25/1, in a race as prestigious and full of class runners as the 2000 Guineas, had absolutely no chance of winning and that they were 'throwing their money away'.

Cockney Rebel won, of course, by one and a half lengths, and from another horse that had high odds going into the race, while the favourite, Adagio, the nag I'd put my money on, took his time and eventually wandered over the finish line in 12th place.

Those couple of days we spent in Newmarket that year were fun for all sorts of reasons, not least because they gave anyone who happened to wander in and have a look at what was going on the opportunity to throw some darts and get involved in a little competition with myself and some of the others who were there with me. One of them was a lad by the name of Spencer Clay, who got in touch with my co-author Edward Couzens-Lake, to tell him a little bit about that day. We are both happy to include his memories below.

Spencer's Story

A few of us had gone along to the Newmarket races for the Guineas Festival. Part of the package we had included special tickets for a marquee tent that was hosted by one of the bookies who were involved with the Guineas at the time. We went to take a look inside and found Keith Deller and Eric Bristow standing at the entrance and asking people if they wanted to enter the darts tournament they were hosting.

We all agreed that we'd give it a go – although we'd had no idea beforehand that such an event was taking place as there'd been no mention of it anywhere. Inside the marquee, there was a stage, on which was a dartboard where, throughout the meeting, and primarily between races, people had been invited to throw nine darts. It was very popular and I reckon that several hundred people all had a go, including Lester Piggott and John McCririck. Someone was keeping all the scores as everyone was told the four people who'd got the highest scores with nine darts would be invited back to compete in a Pro-Am tournament with one of the legends who was there on the day. One of them, as it happened, was me, but only just; I sneaked into fourth place with a score of 196 with my nine darts, which was nothing special but enough to get me into the Pro-Am.

I was paired with Keith while my best mate Dave Ewens, who'd also qualified, was teamed up with Eric Bristow, with Cliff Lazarenko and Bob Anderson the other professionals involved.

The Pro-Am was played as 501 and was the best of five legs. Keith and I beat Bob Anderson and his partner in our semi-final which meant that we'd end up facing Eric Bristow and Dave in the final.

I checked out with a double ten in the first leg to put us one up, then Keith checked out with double 12 to put us 2-0 ahead. We then played the third leg and, inevitably, it all came down to me and a moment that I will never forget, as, giving it the full tournament treatment, I stepped up and heard Russ Bray saying, 'Spencer, you require 116.' I managed the treble 20 and followed up with a single 16 so, by then, I was visibly shaking but, somehow, managed to hit double top to win. That meant Keith and I had beaten Eric and Dave 3-0 and I ended up being mobbed by all of my mates on the stage.

The prize that was provided by the bookies was absolutely top notch – a trophy, plus a weekend for four in a four-star hotel in Blackpool as well as tickets for the semi-finals and final of the World Matchplay that was being held there. But that wasn't all. I also got £500 spending money and £500 of betting vouchers as well as access to the players' VIP bar with free food and drink, our travel expenses paid and a table and seats directly behind the board for all of the matches.

It was an unbelievable weekend, sat there in the players' bar and chatting to Keith, Phil Taylor, James Wade and Terry Jenkins, plus, of course, Eric Bristow. He and Keith were always great company and what a character Eric was. When I got home, I sent the boss of the bookies who'd arranged everything a 'thank you' note, saying what an unbelievable couple of days it had been and how amazing their hospitality had been before adding that I was looking forward to seeing them all again next year.

So, imagine my delight when they got back in touch with me, saying that if I contacted them a month or so before the event, they'd send me some tickets, something which they ended up doing for a further three years after that – talk about my milking it.

I ended up doing the darts event at Newmarket again the following year and, that time, was the top qualifier of the four with a score of 380. It wasn't to be second time around though, as, paired with Eric, we lost the semi-final.

A few years later, I was sat in a waiting room in a West Suffolk hospital, reading a *National Geographic* magazine. I happened to look up from it as someone else entered the room and sat down – it was Keith Deller, my playing partner at Newmarket from what was now quite a few years earlier.

'All right Keith?' I said.

His response will forever be etched into my brain.

'Spencer Clay, as I live and breathe.'

I couldn't believe it. After all of that time, Keith had remembered my name.

It all sounds rather far-fetched when its written down like this and people usually think I'm bullshitting when I tell the story. But I'm sure Keith will corroborate it. And what a great guy he is. I will always be thankful to Keith, Eric and Russ Bray for helping me to have all of those wonderful memories. I know they might not mean much to other people but, for me, it was massive, still is. Great times.

Thanks again Keith. And good luck with the book.

* * *

Another exhibition I remember well took place in the rather more prosaic surroundings of a Yorkshire club. I like, on such nights, to get to the venue for about 5.30pm so I can get some practice in as well as meet and socialise with some of the locals. However, the only bar at the club was for men only, and I was duly advised that Kim was not allowed to come in.

'OK,' I said. 'I'm off to find a pub where my wife is allowed to come in with me.'

Which is what we did. Meanwhile, the club, which was expecting 700 people there that night, started to fill up but, by 7.55pm (the exhibition started at 8pm) and with no sign of me anywhere, the organisers were starting to get a little bit nervous. I eventually showed up just before the start time, only for one of the club's committee members to accost me, saying, 'Where 'ave yew bin?'

'I was here two and a half hours ago,' was my reply before heading in and starting to play, beating some of Yorkshire's top players in the process. And, to be fair, it was a great night in the end. It was a long trip up there but we'd while away the time by listening to Steve Wright on the radio while, on the way home, I'd do my usual thing and fall asleep while Kim chilled out listening to the likes of Dr Hook, Gladys Knight and the Pips and Gloria Estefan.

That was one of the great things about exhibitions (no, not Kim's taste in music), the fact that I never really knew what to expect, as the venues and people who ran them were all so different. I'd have no idea about who I'd be playing against either, until they got up on to the stage and, while there was always a good mix of players, ability-wise, some of them were actually very good and we'd end up having a very decent game, which was great for me as it meant I was, in effect, being paid to practise. On one occasion though, the pub that the brewery had sent me and Bobby George to didn't seem to know much about darts. The staff were well meaning and, as was nearly always the case, nice people, but their dartboard was on the back of the men's toilet door, which wasn't ideal. I initially thought that they'd quickly put one up there so some of their regular punters could get a little extra practice in, so I asked the landlord where we'd be playing the exhibition only for him to respond by wordlessly pointing at the aforementioned toilet door.

I had 16 players taking me on that night and, after every three games, we'd take a five-minute break. During one of those breaks, I walked up to Bobby, who was enjoying himself as usual and asked him what was going on. His response was typically to the point but it also made a lot of sense to me as well.

'Keith, as long as the cheque goes in the bank, it's job done.'

The cheque for that night did go in the bank, so, whatever I might have thought about that particular pub's facilities, it was, as Bobby said, job done and move on to the next one. I swiftly learned to expect the unexpected and to just get on with the job, reasoning that if everyone there ended up having a great evening then that was all that mattered, a philosophy I still take with me to my shows to this day.

* * *

One tour I won't forget in a hurry was my first in the Republic of Ireland. I'd done a few shows in Northern Ireland and, perhaps naively, thought the arrangements would be pretty much the same across the border with the shows always starting at 8pm. My tour in the Republic of Ireland was ten days long so, right at the start, I asked the promoter what time I'd be picked up in order to go to the venue. His reply was that my first night would be at a club that was around an hour's drive away. Which was great; time, I decided, for me to have a couple of beers in the hotel bar before getting into the car at about 6pm and at the club for 7pm. I duly arrived at the club at that time and, from then until 9pm, was sat at the bar there drinking on my own with hardly anyone else in the place. Then someone did arrive, the promoter, so I had a few words with him.

'This isn't exactly the start I wanted on this tour.'

He looked a bit put out at my words before replying, a little defensively, 'All 150 tickets were sold and they'll be in here for 10.30pm, ready for you to start at 11.'

I couldn't believe it.

'Eleven? Starting at 11? Why on earth did you get me in here so early if we're not starting until then?'

His expression now changed from put out to incredulous.

'Because you told me to.'

Kim enjoyed (I hope) six non-stop years on the road with me until we had Lauren, our first child, which is when she said she'd now just accompany me to Las Vegas every year, a destination that we are both very fond of where we spent our honeymoon.

Kim had to put up with a lot in the early days of our marriage, not least in 1986 when my game was so up and down. I never really knew what sort of darts I'd be playing until I was stood at the board and throwing them – regardless of whether I was practising, having a friendly game with some mates or playing in a tournament. I'd play like you'd expect a former world champion to play one moment and look more like the reserve for the Dog & Duck team the next.

The year didn't start well for me at the World Championship, which was being played at the Lakeside Country Club in Frimley Green for the first time. I was seeded at five and, after getting over the surprise at not having to play Nicky in the first round (he hadn't qualified; the first time Nicky had missed out in the Worlds since his first appearance there in 1978, when he got to the semi-finals), I put in my usual few hours of practice before my match against Mike Gregory, which I comfortably won 3-0, throwing a three-dart average of 88.05 in the process.

That win gave me a lot of confidence. It was a great start to a new year and, heading into my second-round match against Alan Glazier, I could see a path to the semi-finals and a meeting with Eric was more than possible, a plan of action that soon came crashing down around my ears as Alan beat me 3-1.

And that is pretty much how it was for the rest of that year. Great darts one minute, poor ones the next. Being so inconsistent is, for me, as frustrating as it gets. If I'm playing well then, of course, that's great; getting into a good rhythm and building up your confidence from winning game after game after game is as good a place as there is to be in any sport. You end up being carried along by the momentum and that played an enormous part in my world title win in 1983. If, on the other hand, and this may well be the case for any professional sportsman or woman, you are playing badly then yes, that is about as bad as it gets. But there is, even in that dark place, the hint of a silver lining and better things to come, because you know that you can only improve and that the only way to go is onwards and upwards. There's a famous saying in sporting circles that claims, 'Form is temporary, class is permanent,' and I'd subscribe to that for darts. You can be having an absolute stinker at the board but, deep down, if you've been at the very top of the game then you don't have anything to prove to anyone and you know that you'll be able to work your way back up to the heights you'd previously attained. It's a realistic belief and we've all been there.

But being inconsistent, blowing hot and cold, checking out on 138 one day and missing out on 52 the next? That's the worst thing of all, because you then don't know where your game is at all and start to ask questions. One second you might be thinking of being the world champion again, the next you're wondering if you're going to have to go through the qualifiers just for the right to be there. I hated it and, for that reason, the first nine months of 1986 are, to be honest with you, a bit of a blur to me, a time best forgotten. Until, that is, I travelled up to Redcar for that year's British Professional Championship in September and, from the first leg of the first set in my opening match against Eddie Garrett, I felt as if I was going to do well. Which was great, as I hadn't really expected anything from the tournament other than doing well enough to keep my ranking high enough to make sure I qualified for the next World Championship. I beat Eddie 3-2 and, although that sounds close, I was never in any doubt, not for a second, that I wouldn't win the match and, as we shook hands at the end, I couldn't help but think I had a chance as I hadn't felt this good at a tournament for ages.

I beat Robert McKenzie 4-1 in the next round before winning 5-3 against Mike Gregory in the quarter-finals. Mike had already shown he was a top player by then, getting to the final of the World Masters in 1983 before really pushing on the following year, winning the British Professional Championship, the Butlin's Grand Masters and the British Matchplay. That's an impressive treble by any standards. He'd even won the Finland Open that year so now, two years on, Mike was a big name in the sport who knew what it was like to win titles. So while this wasn't exactly a make-or-break encounter for me as far as my game was concerned, it would, after a forgettable year so far, at least give me an idea of where I was and, critically, help me work out if I'd left that run of inconsistency behind and could now, once again, be considered as one of the world's best players. I certainly felt that way afterwards. I beat Mike 5-3 and now faced Jocky Wilson for a place in the final.

To say I never turned up for that match would be one of the great understatements of my career so far. Jocky was never in the slightest bit troubled by me. He won it with a double 16 and, after celebrating with his legions of fans, gave me what he probably thought was a friendly pat on the back in sporting sympathy – except he ended up whacking me on the back of the head in his joy at winning and, let me tell you now, you didn't want to be hit by Jocky even if he was in a good mood, never mind a bad one. That friendly little slap ended up stinging quite a bit. If you look back at that match now, you'll notice, simply by the expression on my face, just how fed up I was at the moment of defeat, so much so that, the first thing I said to Kim as she came to console me afterwards was short and to the point, 'We're going home now.'

And no, Kim didn't have any say in the matter. It felt like my exit from the World Championship in 1984 all over again, a heavy defeat and me reacting by just wanting to get the hell away from the darts, the venue, the people there, everything. It took us five hours to get home and I can't even say that I was scintillating company on the journey either, as I slept for most of it and had, believe me, a lot of grovelling to do to a very angry wife over the days that followed.

Kim didn't deserve that. She has supported me from day one and isn't a 'stay at home' partner either – if she can join me and be there at a tournament, she will be. It makes a lot of difference if, at the end of a tough day, you aren't heading off to a lonely hotel room and room service but instead the company of a loving wife. So I think it's only fair for me to give her an opportunity to have her say at this point, what it has been like being married to me, and, for better or worse, living, sleeping and breathing darts for the last three and a half decades or so.

Kim's Story

I was very much my own person when Keith and I first met. I'd left school, gone to work and began to build up a bit of career progression for myself. My first job was with a local branch of the NatWest bank and I didn't like it at all. For starters, I was stuck in what they referred to as the 'machine room', which was not only very noisy but, because of the security involved, had no windows. We weren't even allowed to talk to one another and even if you were in a part of the building where you could chat, the senior employees at the bank didn't want to have anything to do with the youngsters, they pretty much ignored us, so, for me, it was a working environment that was even worse than school.

But it made me strong and want to have something better for myself. So, when the opportunity came along to work for the Leeds Permanent Building Society as a cashier, I was only too happy to take it. The role was in a much more enjoyable atmosphere and, importantly, it gave me a lot of confidence around people. Which is where I was, life- and work-wise, when I first met Keith. He'd been invited to my brother's wedding as my sister-in-law is the niece of Olly Croft, who was the founder of the BDO. Olly's son was a good friend of Keith, hence him being invited.

I knew who he was at the time, but that was all. We'd all been keeping an eye on that first World Championship he entered and I remember saying at the time, as he made his way into the quarter- and semi-finals, 'Let's hope the young one wins.'

Little did I know how things would eventually end up.

When we met at the wedding, it felt, for me, as if we'd known each other for a long time. He was charming, very easy to talk to and good company. He had to rush off and play in a tournament soon afterwards but there was no immediate urgency about anything. I think we knew we'd soon meet up again and could pick up from there. So we ended up exchanging telephone numbers but, rather than trying to be all cool about it, as most of us tried to be at the time, like not bothering to call or telling whoever answered the phone when he rang to tell him I was out, we ended up just wanting to be with each other whenever we got the opportunity.

Keith has always, from day one, made me feel very secure about him and how he treated me and about our relationship. A lot of the players, for one reason or another, didn't want their wives or girlfriends to come with them to wherever they were playing but Keith wanted me to be at as many tournaments as possible. These might have ended up being quite expensive for him, especially some of the smaller events. Take, for example, something like the Finnish Open where I'd worked out he would need to get to at least the semi-finals in order to break even. So the money, what little there was of it at those contests, was important but what was far more important to Keith was the ranking points you got at each one, depending on how well you did. One ranking point might not sound very much but it was enough to make a big difference, depending on whether you got it or not.

Keith is a very romantic man and very protective of me. I remember when we started going out with each other someone from the press rang him and said I was already engaged to someone else. That was a load of nonsense. But if someone wanted a story, it didn't mean they'd always go to him for it. I was at work one day when someone came to the counter and said they were from *The Sun* and asked if I would go for a drink with them at a local pub over my lunch break.

I couldn't believe it. There was no way I was going to do that and I told the chief clerk that I was being bothered by a reporter, so he soon got rid of her. But it didn't end there. Later that same day I had to go to hospital as I'd been in a minor car crash and my mum was worried I might have whiplash. We were there for hours but never saw anyone and, eventually, came home again. I got out of the car and, just as I was about to go through our garden gate, two men appeared from nowhere and one of them started asking me questions as he blocked my way to the gate. So I had to get my dad to get rid of him. It wasn't a very nice experience and it made me realise that being involved with someone like Keith, who was very much in the public eye at the time, was going to have moments like that.

Keith was in Spain at the time and with there being no mobile telephones I couldn't just ring and tell him what had happened, not straight away. I knew, however, that he'd probably see all the newspapers the next day, even if he was in Spain, so I was frightened about what they might say and how he would have responded. I ended up going to stay with my brother and, a little while later, after I'd been with Keith in Cornwall for an exhibition and up in Scotland for a tournament, I remember telling my mum, soon after we got back, 'I'm just going to go over and stay with Keith for a bit and help him get straight again and give him a hand with his washing and ironing' – and that was it, I never moved out again after that. He didn't want me to be bothered by the press again so I was either with him at his place or at whatever event he was at.

I wasn't the only partner who became part of the 'tour'. Eric Bristow's partner, Maureen, was always with him, as was Carol, Cliff Lazarenko's wife. Mind you, she didn't just come along to keep Cliff company – he didn't drive so she drove him everywhere just as, to be fair, I have, and do, for Keith. He's probably mentioned already how he wanted to come straight home after he was knocked out of the British Professional Championship in 1986. Well, we did but he did at least read the map so we could work out how to leave Redcar and get on to the A1 before he went to sleep – and when he did, I thought, 'Thank God for that, I can have a little bit of peace and quiet now.' He'd been so down and I understand why, but it was beginning to wear me out a bit. The funny thing is, the next day we'd swapped roles, so to speak. Keith was all upbeat, optimistic and ready for anything again, while I was a bit down and depressed. But he did his bit to try to get me out of it again.

He'd be like that; he can be very full-on and intense when he's in the mood. Even now, when he spends a lot of his time promoting and working with some of the younger players, he'll sort out a booking for them and get an enormous amount of pleasure in just giving them a call and saying, 'I've sorted something out for you if you're interested?'

But it doesn't end there for him. He'll then do everything he can to make sure that booking, whatever it is, is a success – he'll be checking on ticket sales and things like that. It'd be nice if some of the people he's done all this for were a bit more appreciative of his time and effort than they have been. But that's Keith, he just wants to help. We've worked together on his darts and career right from the start – and he is, at least, very appreciative of all the work I have done for him. We're a good team; his strengths are my weaknesses and vice versa. I'm his PA really I suppose. I know how the sport works. Half of the year is, or certainly was, devoted to all the tournaments, from September through to January, culminating in the World Championship. The other part of the year was doing the exhibitions and whatever work Keith got through the breweries, which was, as Eric so aptly described, the 'bread and butter' work.

I must mention one of the other great loves in Keith's life and that's Sheba. She was the very first German Shepherd we ever had and, before we had children, Sheba went absolutely everywhere with us. We'd have taken her with us to events if we'd been able to, but thought it was probably a little bit more sensible to leave her behind with my mum and dad when we did. Sheba loved sport as well. Keith and I would be playing a little bit of pitch and putt until Sheba came along and helped herself to all the golf balls – so that was the end of the game. We'd go out and have a game of tennis and she'd sit and watch us for a while before she got bored – so that would be the end of that as well as she chased after the balls as we played. She'd even run after a football if Keith was having a kick-about, sink her teeth into it and puncture it. She was a great companion and we've had two more since. We just love having a dog about the place as they help to ground you. You can never worry too much about the next match or tournament if there's a dog around.

Keith is now looking forward to the pending (at the time of writing) World Seniors Darts Championship in 2022 – so excited, in fact, he's like a kid at Christmas about it. So I'll be going along to that with him. It'll be, knowing some of the names who are lined up to play, very competitive indeed, and he'll want to win it. But I'm sure they'll all have some fun as well. The sport was so cut-throat in the early days of his career. Matches that were the best of only three sets, if you started poorly in your first match you might be out and on your way home before you'd even hung your shirts up in the hotel room. So he'll enjoy this one as will, I am sure, everyone that goes along to watch it. But that's Keith really, he just wants people to be happy and to have some fun in life and it's a joy to be part of that with him.

* * *

Despite that heavy defeat to Jocky Wilson at the British Professional Championship that year, I was, as far as a venue is concerned, really beginning to like spending time at Redcar, which is a lovely little seaside town a few miles east of Middlesbrough on the North Sea coast – even if it was a bit of a trek in the car to get there. So, despite being sent home by Jocky in a bad mood, I knew that I was more than capable of going a step further the following year and winning the title. It's one that all the professionals wanted to win and, after the World Championship, was probably regarded as the second most prestigious on the tour.

That meant my 1987 was really focused on that tournament rather than the World Championship, although with that now taking place at Frimley Green in Surrey it was not quite as bad a commute for me. I'd just sneaked my way into the rankings there as number eight, which meant I was in the top half of the draw and would be up against the Welsh player Brian Cairns in the first round. Brian was 47 and this was his first appearance in the World Championships, giving him a match against a former winner in his first match. No pressure there, Brian. And there wasn't. I think he must have gone in regarding it as a bit of a 'free hit' as no one would have been surprised if he'd lost so he just set out to have a go and enjoy himself. If that was his policy, it worked very well as Brian dealt with the match and surroundings very well, seeing me off 3-0. That meant another early exit for me, another disappointingly early departure from the biggest event on the tour and, again, another quiet drive home for Kim as I slumbered in the passenger seat. But I wasn't too down as I reckoned that, come September, I'd be more than ready to give the British Professional Championship a go.

I beat Peter Locke 3-0 in the last 32, a convincing win that gave me an extra boost of confidence. Everything now seemed as if it was falling into place. I was in a good mood after a straightforward win, I liked the venue and, with next taking on Steve Parkes – someone I knew I was capable of beating – I could see a path to the final opening up ahead of me.

I beat Steve 4-2. So, job done and I was in the quarter-finals where I'd be up against Peter Evison. Peter was still a bit of an unknown quantity back then but he was a very good player who'd knocked out John Lowe at Redcar the previous year, so he was going to be a tough opponent. I needed to be on my game from the start and I was, winning 5-2. With that victory and a place in the semi-finals now assured, I reckoned the only player left who'd be capable of giving me a good game was Jocky, the man who'd sent me crashing out at that stage a year ago.

The draw was set up so that Jocky and I would meet at that stage again and I was more than ready to have my revenge until, much to everyone's surprise, not least myself, Jocky lost to Ronnie Sharp in his quarter-final, which meant I'd now be taking on Ronnie for a place in the final.

Ronnie, or 'Pancho' as he was known in the game, was from Dundee and was the captain of Scotland's national team. So he probably didn't particularly enjoy knocking Jocky out so early and would, I am sure, have much preferred to have had an all-Scotland final against him. But he was going to have to sort out a Sassenach instead, who he had beaten earlier in the year at an event that had been set up for the regional TV company Tyne-Tees to broadcast. Anyway, Ronnie now clearly felt that winning against me in that match meant he was the red-hot favourite to do the same thing again in Redcar and he was, I have to say, a little cocky going in, looking at me straight in the eyes as we were being introduced to the crowd by the MC immediately before the match, saying, 'I can't wait to play you.'

He might have thought that attempt at a touch of pre-match psychology would have had a negative effect on me but, if anything, it pumped me up even more. I really wanted to beat him, and, giving him the Deller equivalent of the hard stare, I said, 'It's the same for me Ronnie, because if I'd been playing against Jocky now, it'd be a much harder game.'

Pre-match verbals before the darts, who would have thought it.

When Ronnie had beaten me earlier in the year, it had been a best of three sets format. That, for me, is the darts equivalent of T20 in cricket – short and sharp, an opportunity to get a lot of big scores quickly and see off your opponent before he's even got into his rhythm. A longer match would suit me and, although Ronnie's 5-4 win over Jocky had given him a lot of confidence going into our game, I reckoned he'd peaked with that win and I'd be able to take advantage. I also, it has to be said, wanted to shut him up, which I was able to do as I started playing some of the best darts of my career to date, racing into a 4-0 lead, only needing two more sets to make another major final. I was hitting everything I needed to, he looked completely shell-shocked and, although he managed to take one set from me, I won 6-1 and, as we left the stage, I couldn't help but offer him a few more words to reflect upon as he packed his bags, 'You won't look forward to playing me so much next time, will you Ronnie?'

There's confidence and there's over-confidence. Ronnie had been hit by a severe case of the latter and had forgotten he was playing the man who was ranked number eight in the world. I'd very much enjoyed reminding him who I was that afternoon. He was still a good player, mind you. Ronnie made his first appearance in the World Championships in 1990 and got to the quarter-finals, beating John Lowe en route.

Then, in 1994, after the leading BDO players left to form the WDC (later the PDC), Ronnie found himself one of the leading BDO players left in the contest and made it all the way to the semi-finals before losing 5-1 to John Part, the eventual champion. In doing so, he became the first and, as it turned out, only player to take a set from John in the 1994 BDO World Championship, denying John what would have been a remarkable achievement in winning the title without losing a single set.

All of that was to come. What mattered in the here and now was that I'd got to the final, something which, as far as this particular tournament was concerned, had been one of my major objectives right from the start of the year. My opponent was Leighton Rees, the gentle giant from Ynysybwl in Wales. Leighton was, like me, a former BDO world champion having won it back in 1978 after beating John Lowe so, from the tournament organisers' point of view, it was probably as good a final match-up as they could have got.

The funny thing is however, that even though he'd reached the final, Leighton wasn't even meant to be at that tournament in the first place. He'd been drafted in as a last-minute replacement for Alan Evans who had, unfortunately, been admitted to hospital just before it began. So there was no pressure on Leighton who was able to go along, catch up with some mates and just enjoy his darts, with nothing expected of him. He was now in the final and the whole thing was a real darts fairy story in the making as he hadn't won any of the major tournaments since his BDO success nearly a decade earlier. On top of that, his game hadn't been at its best in the years that had followed either; he'd exited the Worlds at the first-round stage in four of the previous six years, while in the other two he hadn't even qualified. In the British Professional Championship he'd made the second round in 1983 but had gone out in the first round in 1982, 1984 and 1985 while in 1986 he hadn't entered. So, at 47, those recent few days had been a bit of playing renaissance for Leighton, with a return to top-class competition and, in all probability, in front of a large proportion of the BBC audience who didn't even know who he was.

There I was, the man who was out to spoil the fairytale for him and everyone by beating him in the final.

I wanted to win. But all of a sudden I found that I had even more incentive to do so as I'd discovered that the producer of the BBC coverage of the tournament was Mike Adley, who was also the producer of *A Question Of Sport*, my favourite television programme at the time. This was an opportunity I couldn't miss, so I had a quick word with Mike shortly before the final.

'When can I come back on the programme then?'

Mike's answer was just what I wanted to hear.

'Win the final and I'll have you on Sunday week.'

Leighton and I went on to have a great match, which I won 7-5, and, while it felt great to have won the British Professional Championship for the first time (plus a cheque for £10,000), I now found myself almost as excited by the fact I was due to go back on to *A Question Of Sport*. It was a good show too, featuring golfer Ian Woosnam, who'd just collected a substantially bigger cheque, £1m to be exact, after winning a tournament at Sun City in South Africa, and cricketer Mike Gatting who was, at the time, as famous for having a run-in with the umpire Shakoor Rana as he was for being captain of the England team. It was a good show which attracted an audience of 14 million viewers.

Fourteen million viewers. Things were going well for the lad who used to make up boxes that the freshly made cakes went in.

7

Changes

What more could I do? The situation felt hopeless

PICTURE THE scene. Darts is, for once, completely off the menu. It's March 1991 and I'm relaxing at home, watching the film *Dirty Rotten Scoundrels* with Kim and we're laughing away as the aforementioned scoundrels, Freddy and Lawrence (played by Steve Martin and Michael Caine), are attempting to con their way to riches. Laughing, that is, until Kim sat up and said, 'My waters have broken.'

Off we went to the local hospital where, a short time later, Lauren, our beautiful daughter, was born. It had been a tough birth for Kim as Lauren wasn't in too much of a hurry to make an appearance, so much so in fact that, in the end, Kim had a ventouse (this requires the use of a cup-shaped device that can be attached to the baby's head in order to assist with the birth) delivery and, at 8.47am precisely, Lauren finally came into the world.

Only those of you who have experienced the joy of being a dad for yourself will know that feeling of utter joy when you hold your newly born child for the first time.

Lauren wasn't an only child for too long though, as our wish to have a girl and a boy was fulfilled a short time afterwards when Matthew was born. He comes with me to all the darts tournaments and is referred to as Matty by all the other players.

Life is never the same when you become a parent. But my life had, already, been changing as far as the game and my part in it was concerned over the previous few years.

Winning the British Professional Championship in 1987 had been another career high point for me. It was the one title that, after the Worlds, I'd been most keen to win. I now felt as if I'd done something of a darts double, winning two of the biggest tournaments in the game within four years, which was quite an achievement, especially given the quality of opposition around at the time as well as the calibre of players who were now coming through and threatening the 'old guard' in the process.

So 1988 became the last year that I played in all the major events. It didn't start particularly well for me as I went out of the World Championship in the first round, losing 3-1 to John Lowe. I didn't have a ranking going into that tournament while John was seeded as two, so, from being one of the big names and getting what you might call a fairly comfortable draw in the first two rounds or so, I was now one of the players who the seeds were coming up against and expecting to beat. Having said that, I don't think for one second that John saw he was up against me and expected to win. I was probably the one unranked player who none of the other competitors wanted to come up against. But not having a ranking hurt me. My win in the British Professional Championship only counted for British, rather than world ranking points, so I had to a certain extent slipped out of things a little bit.

* * *

I came back to defend my British Professional title in 1988 and got as far as the quarter-finals, winning against Cliff Lazarenko and John Goves, but then lost a thrilling last-eight match 5-4 to Dave Whitcombe. I was particularly disappointed about that as, had I won, I would have been up against Jocky Wilson in the semi-finals and we'd always enjoyed a great rivalry. But it wasn't to be on this occasion.

I needed to catch up so I'd been playing in all of the ranking events to do so. But I went out of the World Masters in the second round and the World Matchplay in the first round. So picking up the ranking points I needed wasn't happening for me. At the same time, the exhibition work, which Eric Bristow valued highly and, as Kim said earlier on in this book was our 'bread and butter', was starting to dry up.

I was, at the time, with the management team of McLeod Holden Enterprises Ltd and a manager, Dick Allix, who, as well as looking after me, also handled both Eric and Cliff. I did feel, at this time, that I had a place in the pecking order as far as Dick was concerned which meant that I would, at least, get the work that Eric and Cliff couldn't do, but, for one reason or another things never quite worked out and it never turned out to be the successful partnership I'd expected it to be. Dick told me I needed to improve my world ranking in order to get more work but, even when I did that, there was still nothing for me. I was then told I'd get the work I wanted if I won a televised tournament yet, after I'd won the British Professional Championship, there was still no commercial work available for me to take on.

What more could I do? The situation felt hopeless. I wasn't living that comfortable a life. There were always bills to pay, so I needed this work to put food on the table and keep a roof over our heads. That is exactly why Eric called it the 'bread and butter' of our profession. He was right. But, at that time, I didn't even have a crust to call upon, let alone any bread and butter. I was now entering tournaments with only one thing in mind: the prize money that was available, which was not a very good thing to do and certainly went against everything I believed in from a professional point of view.

I decided to ask McLeod & Holden if I could find my own work as they were not being particularly proactive in finding anything for me. They agreed to this, on the proviso that I paid them 20 per cent of whatever fee I was paid as a result of securing work for myself independently and without any input from them, which I agreed to do. That sounds wrong and it was but, by then, I was in a near desperate situation so had no choice but to agree to pay them a commission for doing absolutely nothing. But, as challenging as all of this was turning out to be, there was at least one silver lining in among all of the darkness of that time, which was that I was, gradually, moving away from being purely a competitor and into player management, albeit for myself. This was something that was, certainly in darts, almost completely unheard of back then, with the only player on the circuit who managed himself back then being John Lowe.

Going against what was expected of me didn't go down very well with some people. I remember one particularly tense phone call with Peter McLeod from McLeod & Holden who said to me, 'Don't bite the hand that feeds the mouth.' Not long after that call, I received a letter from him that pulled absolutely no punches and concluded by informing me that my contract with the business had been terminated. It was a cold and blunt letter which further advised me that I was 'no longer a viable client'.

He'd made me feel like a piece of discarded office furniture.

Yet all of this ended up being one of the best things that had ever happened to me. It didn't take me very long at all to discover that I was really good at getting exhibition work for myself, so much so that my diary, which had been blank and unused for so long, was now beginning to fill up. In addition to that and, very significantly, contacts and clients alike all admitted that they preferred dealing with me direct anyway, so much so that I established a lot of long-term and mutually fruitful business relationships in no time, many of which are still in place to this day.

Kim was a great help to me at the time as she kept on coming up with the sort of great ideas that I wasn't getting from anywhere or anyone else, and we ended up becoming a great team. Kim had, for example, been reading a newspaper and had noted that someone had won a big prize while playing bingo.

That was a light bulb moment for both of us. I got on the phone and contacted Mecca, Top Rank and Gala. They were all more than interested in having me come along to one of their big nights and, in the end, I made over 100 appearances at bingo halls all over the country.

Later on, I started appearing at lots of Suffolk's holiday camps – Butlin's and Pontins for example. This was courtesy of Colin Deaton, so via Colin I started to do three appearances a week on the Isle of Wight, along with my dad, who came with me. The venue on the island certainly had a wide repertoire of outside guests as, in addition to me, they'd also book in table tennis players and wrestlers. All of us had the use of the same car while we were there. The keys were left under the driver's seat and whoever used the car last would park it back up and leave the keys there for the next person. That worked well until the day I was heading down a hill in the car and the brakes failed, meaning that I ended up, along with the car, in the bushes at the side of the road. So that was the end of that. I ended up leaving the car there and, along with Dad, got the train and ferry home. But, having said that, not all of my appearances at the country's holiday centres were quite as hazardous. Take, for example, Potters near Great Yarmouth, which is – among other things – famed for hosting the World Indoor Bowls Championships since 1999. John Potter, the owner, is a good friend of mine and I have to say, he runs a magnificent place. Potters has been, and remains, in a different class to all of the other holiday centres I have worked at.

Maybe my adventures up and down the country, all down to the sole efforts of Kim and myself, were exactly what McLeod & Holden had feared would happen. If one darts player suddenly found it was turning out to be far more profitable for him or her to go their own way, then maybe Eric Bristow, Cliff Lazarenko and a lot more would end up doing the same thing?

I felt certain, at this time, that big changes were coming to the game. The players were becoming more and more well known while the television audiences showed no signs of dropping. If anything, they were on the up. Television's growing interest in the sport had become very apparent back in 1980 when the cover of *Radio Times* featured the pending World Championship, which was starting on 2 February with a huge picture of a dartboard prominently shown. At the time, *Radio Times* was the biggest-selling magazine in a country where television continued to be a major event in the nation's houses. The BBC's most popular programme from the previous year, the final episode of the comedy series *To The Manor Born*, reached an audience of nearly 24 million people.

I'd won that same World Championship three years later and, even if the BBC wasn't getting anything like the audiences for it that it had for Penelope Keith and company, enough people watched the darts and talked about it for me to become, for a while, one of the most well known sports people in the country. That win and my rise to fame and relative fortune hadn't been forgotten and I was now able to book myself no end of work on the basis of that as well as my win in the British Professional Championship in 1987.

Kim and I ended up working on my promotional and exhibition appearances as a team. She was very good at marketing while I was more than capable of selling myself, so we did very well between us. We were totally in control of everything that we did, with the added bonus that there was no 20 per cent commission to pay out to anyone.

Another of Kim's thoughts was that we approached as many military bases around the UK as we could in order to see if they'd book me in to do some exhibition work on their sites. This was an inspired idea and I ended up getting work at military locations all over the country, especially in Portsmouth, which is famous for its Royal Navy dockyard. We also contacted social clubs including the British Legion until we realised that I had enough work, and a good mix of it as well, for me to make a good living again.

One drawback, if I can call it that, was that our focus on doing this meant I was no longer playing in any tournaments, so I never made it back into the BDO rankings and had, in time, accepted that my days of playing darts on television were probably over.

Yet, just as I had long suspected would be the case, the game, with or without me, was about to change. This started to come about at the beginning of the 1990s when the BBC, which had been such a loyal supporter of the game, scaled back its tournament coverage and showed only the BDO World Championship at the beginning of each year. This sudden decline in the big televised events made me realise that I was now not the only player who'd be depending more and more on the exhibition circuit as Eric, John, Jocky and Bob Anderson would now be looking to do the same thing themselves. But, for all of that, I knew I'd made one of the best decisions of my life in deciding to manage myself, and I didn't regret it for a second.

Much of my work was with breweries and it was this that had given Kim and I the renewed financial security we felt we needed to have before we started a family. When Lauren came along it was, for me, an exciting time in more ways than one as it meant I needed to find deals that would enable me not only to support Kim and myself, but also my daughter.

I felt as if I'd hit rock bottom when I got that letter from Peter McLeod. The contents had been curt and dismissive, so much so that there were moments when I wondered if I'd ever make my living from playing darts again. But that was then and this was now. I was, with the new direction my career was taking and Lauren's birth, on a complete high. We were helped, at this time, by Alec and Sheila, Kim's parents, who were an absolute godsend as not only did they act as our babysitters whenever Kim and I set off for another exhibition, they also looked after our beautiful German Shepherd, Sheba.

Sheba played a very big part in our lives. And we'd been through a few traumas with her during that time. In around 1987, she needed to have a pioneering operation for a hip replacement at the Royal Veterinary College, which was performed by one of the very few surgeons who was able to do this procedure at the time. This was carried out on one side before, three months later, she had to have the other side done. But, after that had been done, the specialist vet looking after he said he wasn't very happy with how the first operation had gone and that, in his opinion, it needed to be done again – except, on this occasion, it would have to be carried out at our cost.

Some people reacted to that news when we told them that it would surely be 'better' to have Sheba put down and to get ourselves a new dog? We couldn't believe that we were even being asked to consider that option and, even though times were tough back then and it was expensive, we had that operation done as Sheba was part of the family. Alec and Sheila loved Sheba so much that Kim and I decided that we would buy them a German Shepherd puppy for Christmas. But we weren't going to dive straight in and turn up one day, completely unannounced, with a big cardboard box. No, we decided that, given Alec and Sheila already owned Mitzi, who was a Poodle Terrier, we should ask first, so, given that any dog is a big undertaking and commitment, we had a word with Sheila about our plans. She was, and this didn't surprise me at all, ecstatic at the prospect, so much so that we ended up regretting confiding in her as she then didn't get the same surprise that Alec had. Anyway, a couple of days before Christmas that year, it was Kim and I who were excited as we picked the puppy up. Tracey, who is Kim's sister, was also in on the surprise now so she came around the house to see the puppy as she couldn't wait two more days to do so. The big day came and, on Christmas morning, we told Alec to sit down in his armchair, close his eyes and hold out his hands. He later told us he thought he was getting a plant.

* * *

It was 'meant to be' as, even though the puppy had been with Kim and me for a couple of days, she had never settled down and we think she knew that she was only going to be with us in passing and that ours was not her forever home. The look on Alec's face when he saw her was absolutely magic and as it was Christmas, they christened her Holly and she was idolised from the beginning. Holly and Sheba soon became the best of friends, which was great as it meant we felt comfortable about leaving her with Sheila and Alec whenever we were away.

Holly wasn't the last addition to our family though as, in October 1992, Kim and I's little family was made complete when our son Matthew was born. We'd always wanted a boy and a girl so everything had turned out perfectly for us, although a growing family meant I was going to have to go out and get even more work. This was at a time when a lot of the top players were getting extremely restless with the lack of television coverage that the sport was getting. The growing discontent meant that, one way or the other, darts was going to have to change and when the inevitable happened, which led to the much-publicised split in the game, it ended up putting me back on television and back in the sporting spotlight.

8

Making a Comeback

Then, out of the blue, I had a
call from Tommy Cox

DO YOU remember 1993? From a sporting point of view, quite a lot happened. Manchester United won the first Premier League title that May, England lost 4-0 to Australia in cricket's Ashes, Greg Norman won the Open Championship and Stephen Hendry defeated Jimmy White in snooker's World Championship.

Plus, more importantly, Ipswich Town finished that first Premier League season in 16th place.

It was a big year for darts as well, but not in terms of who won what, where and when. No, it was a big year in terms of change. And this wasn't a cosmetic change either but something rather more similar in both impact and concept to the ill-fated attempt in the spring of 2021 by some of the leading football clubs in Europe to break away and form their own league.

A 'darts super league'? In a manner of speaking, yes.

By the early 1990s there was little to no darts being shown on television. Its growth and popularity as a televised sport, predominantly on the BBC, had been helped by the fact that, much as Eddie Waring had been the voice of rugby league, Northumberland-born sports commentator, Sid Waddell, was, through his rich and very characteristic commentary, doing the same for darts. People were taking notice of him and then starting to follow the sport as a result, much as they had done with Eddie. But Sid wasn't a sporting one-trick pony – he was, in fact, a much respected man of academia who in the early 1960s worked alongside some very esteemed professors in both politics and economics at the University of Durham. Then, in 1966, Sid started work as a news journalist at ITV, firstly with Granada and then Yorkshire Television. He even devised and wrote *The Flaxton Boys*, a successful children's series on ITV that ran for three years until 1972.

Something else that ITV did in 1972 was to broadcast the News of the World Championship, which was held at Alexandra Palace in London. Sid, being a member of staff, took up the opportunity to go along as an observer and was immediately taken with some of the personalities on show as well as the game itself. Darts was now being watched, probably for the first time, by millions of people who'd previously seen it as not much more than a pursuit played in the dingy back bars of obscure little pubs and clubs in northern England. Sid reckoned there was a bit more mileage in darts as a form of television entertainment than merely showing the big competitions once or twice a year, so he put together the show *Indoor League*, introduced by another Yorkshire gent in Freddie Truman. The programme also featured other lesser-known sports such as bar billiards, table football and arm wrestling. Yet, out of all those and the other pursuits the programme featured, its most popular segment was always the darts.

By 1976, Sid had been tempted over to the BBC, taking his love of indoor sports with him. This made him a natural choice to be one of the commentators when the BBC, which had taken notice of the growth in popularity of the game, screened the first World Professional Darts Championship in 1978. The BBC had already, by then, turned snooker into a regular television event with the programme *Pot Black* (which started in 1969) so, it was now looking to see if it could repeat its success and growing popularity with its viewers, with darts.

The BBC's commitment to televising darts at the time meant that Sid became a regular feature on the nation's TV screens, commentating on every one of the events that it covered from 1978, including my own World Championship win, up until 1994 when he was, as usual, the voice of that year's BDO final between John Part and Bobby George, which John won 6-0 in what was his first appearance in front of the TV cameras. He wasn't the only one, as that year's event featured 17 debutants out of the total entry field of 32. But the sporting headlines weren't so much about those who were taking part in a World Championship for the first time, they were much more focused on those who weren't there; those players who had, reluctantly, decided to split from the BDO and form their own organisation, the World Darts Council (WDC) as an out-and-out rival to the BDO. The famous names who'd made that move included Phil Taylor, Dennis Priestley, Eric Bristow and John Lowe.

By 1993 I'd dropped out of the top 16 in the rankings so wasn't, as a result, playing in any of the few tournaments that were appearing on television at that time. I'd had my last major tournament-playing year in 1988 when I reached the quarter-finals of the British Professional Championship but hadn't done so well in the other three big tournaments, losing in the first round of both the World Championship and World Matchplay, and the second round of the World Masters. As a result of that, I was having to lean more and more on exhibition work in order to, and I'll be honest with you here, make some money in order to support my family as best I could. Then, from 1989 to 1993, my world ranking was so low that I didn't even qualify for the World Championship, the biggest and most high-profile tournament of the year. This had a knock-on effect. By not qualifying, I wasn't appearing on television. By not appearing on television, I was no longer as prominent a name or face as I had been and, like it or not, commercial partners and sponsors will love you all day long providing you're on the television or making the sports pages on a regular basis. If that profile drops, then their interest in you soon tails off and you find yourself looking for work wherever you can.

But this wasn't just happening to me. All of the game's top players were, by now, getting increasingly disillusioned because the number of events being shown on television had dropped from a high of ten per year to just two. This meant even the top, top players like Eric were no longer getting the commercial opportunities they used to and, in fairness, a lot of us were wondering if the game was heading back to the pubs and clubs from whence it came.

Then, out of the blue, I had a call from Tommy Cox.

His is a name that will be familiar to many lovers of darts all over the world. Tommy had, like so many of us, started to worry about the game's future and wanted to do something about it. He did so by joining forces with Dick Allix and forming, in the process, the WDC, along with 14 of the biggest names in the sport, one of which, as far as he was concerned, was going to be me. So, did I want to be part of it? They'd already been promised major coverage of all the events on Sky but, in addition to that, there was also a chance I'd get some regular work on the channel as an in-house expert who is able to advise the cameras about the next shot a player is going to take, a role known as the 'spotter'. That was an agreement which has certainly worked out as I have now been 'spotting' for Sky for a little over 27 years.

Was I interested? Of course I was.

I did have some initial concerns. The BDO had been good to me over the years, but, not only that, I was close to Olly Croft, the founder of the BDO. Would they, I wondered, take action against me moving to the WDC, could the whole thing go legal and might I, as a result of that, run the risk of losing my house?

Tommy was the personification of calmness as he assured me that there was no chance of that happening.

* * *

When the split happened and throughout all that followed, Rod Harrington worked very hard for us as the players' representative. I was worrying about the possible future implications for myself and the game in general but Rod was great with me, a constantly reassuring presence who even ended up getting all of the players 200 shares each in the new organisation. I ended up selling mine and made some good money out of that deal. Mind you, they'd be worth a few hundred thousand pounds by now. All credit to Rod here though, he did a great job and was eventually asked to join the board of the PDC.

So there it was. With Tommy's backing, 16 top names left the BDO in order to join his newly formed WDC:

Bob Anderson, Eric Bristow, Keith Deller, Peter Evison, Richie Gardner, Mike Gregory, Rod Harrington, Jamie Harvey, Chris Johns, John Lowe, Cliff Lazarenko, Dennis Priestley, Kevin Spiolek, Phil Taylor, Alan Warriner and Jocky Wilson.

None of us were now eligible to play in the 1994 BDO World Championship, hence that year's contest including 17 debutants, including eventual winner John Part. The man who John beat in the final, Bobby George, was a player who Tommy had hoped would join us as part of the WDC, but Bobby chose to stay with the BDO, as did, eventually, Mike Gregory and Chris Johns who both, after agreeing to sign for Tommy, decided to return to the BDO. Unfortunately for both of them, however, if they had entertained any thoughts that they'd be welcomed back like prodigal sons by the BDO, they were mistaken and, whether the BDO meant this as a punishment or not I don't know, but the pair were not invited to play in the BDO World Championship that year, which meant they completely missed out.

I completely understand Mike doing what he did. He, like me, saw being part of what was a very controversial move in the game (it had the same impact as Kerry Packer had on world cricket when he initiated a similar split in the mid-1970s) meant, in retrospect, he ultimately felt more comfortable working alongside the organisation he knew best. Bobby, on the other hand, continued to make the very best of what he had – which is, personality and talent-wise, a hell of a lot! He continued to play in the BDO World Championship until 2002, reaching two finals and a semi-final. Bobby is a great player and someone whose company I always enjoy, a man who has given so much to the game through his sheer joy of life and the showmanship that comes with it. His big entrances make the rest of us look positively dull in comparison, walking on to the stage as the 'King of Darts', draped in all sorts of jewellery and necklaces, wearing a cloak and crown and, more often than not, doing so while holding a candelabra as Queen's 'We Are the Champions' is blasting out over the PA.

You don't get a quiet night in with Bobby and, even though he declined to accept any invitation from Tommy to join the WDC, he's kept busy as one of the big names still with the BDO and had regular work with the BBC at the BDO World Championship right up to 2016, which is when the corporation stopped televising the tournament.

The WDC's first televised event was held in Norwich on October 1992. Not on a national scale mind you, as it was only shown on Anglia TV. Tommy, Dick and John had got a sponsor however, and the event was labelled as the Lada Classic and, fittingly for a first event under a new banner, it had its moments. Phil Taylor was knocked out in the quarter-finals by Dennis Priestley while Eric Bristow lost to Jamie Harvey. They were in good company, however, as I also exited at that stage, beaten by Jocky Wilson. Mike Gregory, prior to his returning to the BDO, won the tournament, beating Dennis in the final and taking home a first prize of £5,000 as well as a brand new Lada car.

So not a bad night's work for Mike really.

* * *

When all the players, BDO and WDC convened for the 1993 BDO World Championship, the WDC players stirred up the pot a little bit by wearing badges that had 'WDC' displayed on them, something which made their new loyalties clear to everyone watching. This didn't go down very well with Olly Croft, the supremo of the BDO, who stated that it was 'advertising' and that, as a consequence, the badges were banned and no player could appear in a televised match if he was wearing one. This didn't go down very well with any of the WDC players who had, by then, pretty much decided they'd be holding their own World Championship the following year. They then issued a statement that said unless the WDC was recognised by Olly and the BDO, they would no longer participate in any BDO tournaments. Olly's response to that was to ban us all from BDO events *sine die*.

One story that has always been told is that many of the players felt that Olly and the BDO were dictatorial and they felt as if they were being ordered around all the time. I personally never had a problem with Olly and we never fell out personally, which was just as well as he was the uncle to Sally, my sister-in-law, so Olly was family to us really. But, as far as a lot of the players were concerned, the decree about them not being able to wear those badges was the final straw. Now we were, as far as the BDO (and, as it turned out, the World Darts Federation as well) were concerned, well and truly out on our own and it looked as if we would have no one to play against other than ourselves as the BDO then issued another statement, declaring that any of their players who competed in a match against one of us, or was even at the same exhibition as a WDC player, would be banned.

Mind you, even during those early 'peak' years of television coverage within the game, the top players still felt that, even though they were the reason for darts increasing in popularity and enjoying growing commercial success, the governing body wasn't really looking out for them. Take being selected to play for your country, for example. That is one of the ultimate honours in any sport, but, in darts, it was an honour that was accompanied by the likelihood that you'd end up losing money while you did it. I know dissenting voices will claim that men and women should be prepared, if need be, to play for their country 'for nothing' – but darts players weren't even doing that; it was costing them money to do so. This was their job, remember. I doubt if someone in any other trade would be happy about being asked to take a week or so out of their working schedule, arrange for travel and accommodation for the whole of that period as well as the two to three days of doing whatever you did as a representative for your country – and then get home at the end of the week out of pocket.

The players were the core reason the game was where it was at that time. End of. Not the administrators, not the men in suits sat at a phone all day arranging this, that and the other and then telling the players where they had to be and at what time. Yet the players had little to no say in how the game was run and, as well as that, were not even allowed to display the names of their personal sponsors on their shirts during tournaments. But they were expected to display the BDO ones, even though they wouldn't be paid a penny for doing so. John Lowe was told he could not display the logo of his sponsor Unicorn during tournaments but would have to have that of another company on his shirt instead and to do so for nothing. For those companies, it made it look as if John, one of the biggest names in the sport in the late 1970s and early 1980s, was endorsing them and they'd enjoy the kudos from being associated with John when that was not the case at all.

Talking of sponsors, back in 1990, I had a sponsorship deal with a local finance company in Bury St Edmunds called Tudor Leasing. I was paid £5,000 (equivalent to just over double that today) as well as being provided with a new and sponsored Vauxhall Calibra. I was very grateful, especially with regard to the car, although I do think Tudor could have done a little bit better with its slogan as the car was emblazoned with the phrase, 'Score With Keith Deller'. Kim and I took the car on one of its first trips with us to a county darts match for Cambridgeshire so, to wind up the lads who were there with me – Peter Evison and Martin Adams – I told her to park it right outside the venue.

There it remained until after the event when, as everyone was saying their goodbyes and heading off home, Kim went to start up my brand new and unashamedly sponsored car only for it not to start, however hard we tried. In the end, we had, much to our embarrassment (and, I am sure, everyone else's amusement) to call the AA out to get us home but even that wasn't the end of the story, as Tudor Leasing went into liquidation shortly afterwards. I had, by then, got to quite like the car, despite it letting me down at exactly the wrong time, so ended up buying it from the receivers.

Sponsorship deals like that were essential for all of the top players at the time of the split as, with TV coverage slowly ebbing away, it was the only real chance we had to make some good money – or, in some cases, enough money to pay the bills and live from month to month without having to worry if you were going to end up heading in the same direction as Tudor Leasing. Yet that lack of coverage meant our profiles were going through the floor. It was a period that will go down as one of the unhappiest in the game's history. Yet, looking back, I wonder what else we could possibly have done. Darts was fast disappearing off the nation's television screens while, at the same time, there were too many top players all trying to make a living on the exhibition side where interest and potential income was also dropping. Darts needed a new lease of life and providing it is exactly what Tommy was able to do. So, while I fully appreciated everything that Olly and Lorna, his wife, had done for the game, which had included them putting up their own money to get the BDO going, darts needed fresh impetus and ideas and, as 1994 dawned, it was very clear that this was exactly what was happening.

Olly passed away at the age of 90 in 2019. He was, despite all that had happened and all the animosity that surrounded darts at the time of the split, a giant of the game, someone who, believe me, played a huge part in my rise to fame as well as that of Eric and lots of others. When we heard of his death, I was moved to write a message on my Twitter account, and what I said back then applies today just as it did back then:

'It's a very sad day for darts with the passing of Olly Croft. If it wasn't for Olly myself and many other darts players would never have been able to fulfil our dreams of playing professional darts. Everyone in the BDO and PDC owes a great debt to Olly.'

The split had led to a lot of bad feeling in the game and, unsurprisingly, people fell out about it. But, despite all of that, it did give darts the new lease of life that it so desperately needed and, looking back, I wonder what might have happened if the break-up had never taken place. Sky Sports came on board, just as Tommy had promised, guaranteeing at least three live events per year, which was a great start. Not long after that, Barry Hearn got involved, and right from the start he knew exactly what needed to be done, identifying the players as the stars of the show and treating us accordingly. He not only got some major sponsors into the game but also, in his very first meeting with all the top players, said to us, 'If you do your bit, I will make you millionaires.' As simple as that. We had no reason to disbelieve Barry as he'd worked wonders with snooker in the 1970s and 80s, launching Matchroom and making stars of Steve Davis, Dennis Taylor and, later on, Ronnie O'Sullivan.

Sky knew what needed to be done as well. That old and tediously familiar juxtaposition between darts and ale-soaked back rooms was as far from the broadcaster's minds as possible when it came to covering darts. Sky introduced the walk-on for the players, injecting some American-style razzamatazz into proceedings from the off. Loud music, glamorous girls, the lot. It might sound a little dated now or even unfashionable but it works and the paying punter loves it; the hype and the build-up is as much a part of darts as the match action itself. Sky had, immediately, changed the image of the game, with the presentation and coverage now a long way away from how it was when the BBC had first televised the world finals back in 1978.

And then there was Phil Taylor.

That brave new world of darts needed a superstar and right on cue, Phil entered the stage. His upbringing was as modest as they came. He'd been making ceramic toilet holders for a living (so he was good with his hands from the off) and had never really done anything much with his two sporting passions, football and darts, until he moved to Burslem. Phil probably wouldn't have known at the time that the pub closest to his new home, the Crafty Cockney, was owned by the one and only Eric Bristow but he would go there for a pint and a game of darts of an evening and, as time passed, became good enough to not only be selected for the county team but to start playing at super league level. Eric had, by now, long taken note of Phil and agreed to sponsor him for a year so that Phil could focus on becoming a full-time professional darts player. Whether Eric saw his time and investment in Phil as a gamble, I don't know, but I suspect not, as Eric would have known a good player when he saw one – the difference being that he saw Phil as being a potentially great one rather than 'just' a good one.

Just as I had done, Phil headed off with Eric to play in the USA. He didn't find it easy at first but, once he'd got into his rhythm there was no stopping him, and that time in the States spent with Eric would have been a wonderful education for him, as good as anyone wanting to make it in the game could have got. By 1990, Phil was ready to play in his first BDO

World Championship and, even though he was unseeded, he steamrollered his way to the final, beating Russell Stewart, Dennis Hickling, Ronnie Sharp and Cliff Lazarenko (5-0) en route.

There was no surprise that Phil would be meeting Eric, his mentor and sponsor, in the final. Talk about fate. What is, perhaps, a little more surprising, is how convincingly Phil beat Eric, 6-1, after they had shared the opening two sets. The student really had, in this case, defeated the master.

By the time of the split, Phil was easily, the biggest name in darts and on his way to being one of the most successful sportsmen ever. He added to his 1990 Worlds win by doing so again in 1992, as well as winning the World Masters in 1990. At his last BDO World Championship in 1993, Phil lost to Kevin Spiolek in the second round but that was just the merest of blips as he went on to dominate the game like no one else had before, or, quite probably, ever will. He was the darts superstar that Sky and the WDC, which, from now on, I will refer to by its current name, the Professional Darts Corporation (PDC), had been looking for.

Let's be honest, Phil has taken darts to another level altogether. He was so dominant in the sport that, a few years ago, Ronnie O'Sullivan, who has been the leading force in snooker for years now, called him the 'master of the masters'. There's no higher praise than that you receive from your peers and for Phil to receive such an accolade from Ronnie said everything, not only about how he dominated the game but the way he went about it. Phil is a true gentleman and the ultimate professional with it.

Phil was, almost on his own, pushing the viewing figures for darts upwards and, for a company like Sky, where the bottom line is, quite frankly, God (and nothing else matters), that was enough to lead to more investment and more tournaments being televised live, along with all the hype and publicity that went with it. That was great for Phil, of course, as it meant he became more and more of a household name and could name his own price to anyone who wanted him to take part in one of their exhibitions or sponsor him. If their offer suited Phil, he'd take it; if it didn't, well, he hadn't anything to worry about, he could just wait for the next one to come along – as it invariably would.

There will be those who'll claim that the rest of us were caught up in all of the 'Taylormania' and were improving both our own profiles and commercial values off the back of Phil's success. I'd disagree with that. Phil is, and I'll say it again, one of, if not the most talented player to ever pick up a set of darts, yet, for all that, it also benefitted him that he was going up against so many talented players.

Take, as just one example, the 1995 PDC World Championship, which Phil won. There were some great players in the field that year, including Cliff Lazarenko, Rod Harrington, Bob Anderson, Dennis Priestley and John Lowe, all of whom, as well as quite a few others, were either ex-world champions, myself included, or were more than capable of becoming a world champion themselves.

That is why Phil was, and is, such a great player, because he would regularly take on, and beat, other very top stars. Let's look at that in a footballing sense. As I write this in the summer of 2021, the best football team in England are Manchester City. No arguments there. But it isn't as if they've achieved all they have against mediocre opposition. They're up against other great teams like Liverpool, Manchester United and Chelsea. So when Manchester City win a Premier League title, it's a great achievement for that reason. If they were up against, and with due respect to these clubs, the likes of Southampton, Crystal Palace and Newcastle every week, they'd still win the championship but it wouldn't, perhaps, be seen as quite such an achievement. As far as darts is concerned therefore, Phil's success is very much a case of the former example there. He was, and remains, a giant among other giants. He was just able to walk that little bit taller whenever he was with them and is the greatest player the game has ever seen, there can be absolutely no doubt about that.

* * *

Sky had got in touch and asked me if I wanted to be part of its TV coverage as a spotter. I was never going to say no to that. This was at the same time as the split and the rise and rise of the PDC, back in 1993. I went along and really enjoyed doing it, hoping I would be asked back – which has been happening ever since, just over 27 years now, which must make me one of Sky's longest-serving sports pundits. My 'office', for want of a better word, is usually a truck parked outside of the venue and my role is to instantly tell the camera crew and director where to look as the darts are being thrown. So, let's say Raymond van Barneveld needs 123 to check out. At that stage of any game, it doesn't help anyone if the camera crew are having to focus their shot on where the dart has just landed, they need to know where it is going to go before it gets there. So, 123 needed. All eyes on Keith Deller. And it's a simple one so I call it out, 'Treble 19, treble 16, double nine' – but even then, it's not that straightforward. What if, for example, Raymond misses the treble 19 at the start and scores single 19? It's my job then to recalculate, immediately, as he can still check out, so I call out 'treble 18, bull' for his next two darts, which will still see him checking out on 123. I have to think quickly but so do the camera crew, who must be able to point at whatever part of the board I've called instantaneously. It's split-second stuff and I love doing it and working for Sky.

Covering the game can be a challenge for the TV people as there are, of course, two people playing and they are going to be on different scores. So you need to 'jump' from one to the other as each comes to the oche and focuses on what they need to do before, immediately, switching back. Let's say, for example, your opponent needs a double top while you are still out there needing a 123 checkout. Well, first of all, how did he or she get that far ahead of you? But there it is, that's the situation. So, there are two cameras covering the game – one will focus on the top half of the board, while the other will take the bottom half. To check out on 123 normally means that treble 19, treble 16 and double nine approach. But say you miss that first treble and score single 19 instead. That means an immediate rethink and the remaining darts now needed are treble 18 and bullseye. But what then, if that treble 18 is also missed and the player hits a single there as well? They've scored 37 now, so they can't check out as there is only one dart left. So I'm going to instruct the director to keep the camera focused on the top half of the board as the player will now be going for treble 18 to score 91, leaving 32 on the board and a double 16 checkout when, or, rather, if they get a second chance.

Managing to keep up?

* * *

And that 123 is just one of any permutation of three-dart finish possibilities from 170 (the highest) down to two, hence that need to be like lightning with the calculations and, very importantly, to be right each and every time. I'm not going to last very long with Sky if someone is on a 141 checkout and I'm not able to say what the route is straight away, I can't say, on air, 'Wait a second, let me work this one out.' It was when he was watching me doing this that the genius that is Stephen Fry said he wanted to see me at work, the results of his visit to the trailer being self-evident in the comments he makes in his foreword to this book.

We eventually decided that another spotter was needed and, for that, I had no hesitation in suggesting my good friend and fellow competitor Eric Bristow for the job. Eric was a brilliant counter, as fast as you can get at working out the permutations needed – but he wouldn't always leave it at that. There are more than a few producers at Sky who, if you ask them about Eric, will say he didn't only want to be the spotter, he also saw himself as the producer and director as well. That was how it was with Eric though and everyone accepted that and he brought a great energy and expertise to the Sky team whenever he worked with us at the big events.

It was also important for me to keep playing, although that meant a few potential problems if I was playing a match in the afternoon, lost and then had to report to do my spotting in the evening session as the team in the truck knew I'd probably be in a bad mood when I arrived to do my shift so, for the first hour or so, they'd always tread very carefully around me until I'd got my defeat out of my system and had my spotting hat on. The Sky team are great to work with and I'm very fortunate to be part of their setup, which is fantastic, no question. I'm now doing some spotting for ITV as well and, in addition to that, I do the live draw every year for the UK Open, which always give me a buzz. The ITV team are also first-class and I enjoy working with them as well.

As far as playing and appearing in the major tournaments and being on television, that is manna from heaven as far as any sponsors you might have are concerned. They could be all sat around the table and wondering whether to renew a deal or not and then, one evening and at peak viewing time, there you are, on television, with millions of people watching you as well as, crucially, taking notice of whatever logo you might have on your shirt or the maker of the darts you are playing with. It's the sort of exposure that makes them want to do business with you. The first big tournament I entered was the 1994 WDC (as it still was then) World Championship, one that was arranged and held as a separate tournament to the BDO's tried and trusted version and commencing on Boxing Day 1993, thus guaranteeing, in principle, a large and sofa-bound audience at home who needed some light entertainment after the excesses of the previous day or so.

This meant a new venue, the Circus Tavern in Purfleet. It's a custom-built entertainment complex that opened in 1974 and turned out to be ideal for a large event such as the one we were about to take part in. The format of the tournament was, however, different to the BDO version as the 24 players involved were put into eight groups of three in what was, to start with, a round-robin tournament, with the winner of each of the eight groups going through to the knockout stages. I was drawn with Kevin Spiolek and Steve Brown, but lost 3-1 to both of them, meaning that the last match in our group, between Kevin and Steve, would determine who went through into the last eight, with Steve convincingly doing so, 3-0. I was disappointed, of course, but it was great to be back on a stage, playing the game I loved and in front of a loud and enthusiastic audience, both at the event and at home. Everyone ended up enjoying themselves, especially Dennis Priestley, who beat Phil Taylor 6-1 in the final.

Later on in 1994, I took part in the World Matchplay, which was sponsored by Proton Cars and held at the Empress Ballroom at the Winter Gardens up in Blackpool, a very prestigious venue indeed. Thirty-two players took part in what was a traditional knockout event with the first and second rounds being decided over the best of 15 legs. I won my first-round match 8-6 against the American Jim Widmayer, setting up a second-round game with another Jim from the States, Jim Watkins – and we ended up breaking a record between us.

It was like that tennis match at Wimbledon in 2010 when one of the sets between John Isner and Nicolas Mahut ended up with a score of 70-68. Sixteen years earlier, Jim and I played the darts equivalent and Jim won 18-16.

That's 34 legs in a match that was meant to be the best of 15, so effectively we ended up playing two games even though it counted as just the one. It went on and on and on, so much so that, at one point, I wondered if it would ever finish. We played for so long that, towards the end, we both started to get a touch of dartitis, something that Jim carried forward into his next match, against Rod Harrington. He was so affected still by our game that he never got going and lost 11-7. I suppose I ended up doing Rod a favour by wearing out his opponent for him.

One funny thing that came out of that match was that it went on for so long into the evening, all the technical staff and other people from Sky, who were covering the event, had to work a lot later and longer than they'd expected to. I was working at the event as a spotter so, when I eventually turned up for my working shift the next day, they gave me a lot of stick for making them all late for their dinners.

The eventual winner was another player from the USA, Larry Butler from Kentucky, aka the 'Bald Eagle', who beat Dennis Priestley 16-12 in the final and, in the process, became the first (and still only, at the time of writing) American player to win a PDC title.

With its hunger for darts growing seemingly by the month, Sky put on a new event in 1995 called the World Pairs, which was held in Scotland. Luckily for me, I didn't have to take on Jocky in front of a vociferous crowd this time and, even more luckily, I was paired with my mate Jamie Harvey, a true Scot and someone, I hoped, would keep the audience on our side. Our walk-on music was 'Take The High Road' which took about five minutes from beginning to end but as it got everyone going, that wasn't a problem, even if I ended up fidgeting as we waited. Jamie and I played well together and ended up having a great tournament, getting to the semi-final where we had to play a one-leg shoot-out against John Lowe and Cliff Lazarenko, beating them and earning a place in the final where we'd be up against Dennis Priestley and Eric Bristow, about as good a pairing as you could get. It ended up being a really close game but, as well as I was playing, Dennis was on great form, playing up to me and the audience in the process, and they narrowly beat us in what was a very entertaining final.

I never like to lose but, on this occasion, I had to look at things in a positive way. Only two years earlier I'd dropped right out of the rankings and was having to work really hard to get work. That phone call from Tommy had made all the difference. Not only was I now one of the founder members and leading players with the PDC, I also had my regular work as a spotter with Sky as well as, when it came to exhibition work with various sponsors, a full diary. Now, as 1995 drew to a close, I had another appointment with the Circus Tavern looming, the 1996 World Championship in which, although I wasn't one of the top-ranked players, I reckoned I had a more than fair chance of doing well.

Once again, the tournament commenced with its group stage and, this time I'd been placed in Group B with Sean Downs and, for the second year running, Kevin Spiolek. Sean and Kevin played each other first, with Sean winning 3-0. That meant, such was the way this format worked, that Kevin was probably already out of the tournament, so I guessed his head might have already dropped a bit by the time he played me in the second match. In any case, I was confident I'd beat him and I did, 3-1, meaning I ended top of the group and ready for the knockout stages where I'd be up against Phil Taylor.

Phil had brushed aside Shayne Burgess and Cliff Lazarenko in winning his group without even dropping a set, so it was pretty clear that he was in form and had the title in his sights. He went on to win it after beating me 4-0, John Lowe 5-1 and Dennis Priestley 6-4 in the final. Phil had won 21 of 26 sets in the tournament, with just five lost.

If people hadn't already realised that Phil was going to be a superstar of the game, then I suspect the penny would, finally, have dropped after those championships.

* * *

Life was good. But, as so many people will know, it has a nasty habit of dragging you down just when you are least expecting it. I'd started 1997 on a relatively good note, again winning my group at the World Championship by beating Kevin (having been drawn against him for the third year running) and Dennis Smith before, once again, coming up against Phil in the last eight. I did at least manage to take a set off him this time in losing 5-1, but he was in imperious form again and won the tournament, once more beating Dennis in the final, this time 6-3. I then took a little time out from my increasingly busy schedule, one that permitted me a treat on 15 February when I went to watch my beloved Ipswich Town play, not knowing that, while I was at the game, Kim's father Alec died from a fatal heart attack at just 57 years of age. What a shock. He was a lovely man, generous to a fault, someone who really would do anything for you and the whole family went into mourning, grieving for a wonderful man who was, and still is, very much missed by us all.

The year closed with, as was tradition, the World Championship – now under the PDC banner, the body having taken over from the WDC. It was held again at the Circus Tavern from 29 December 1997 through to 4 January 1998 with the BDO equivalent, held at Lakeside, following on from 3 January to 11 January meaning that, for a couple of days, two different darts world championships were being played at the same time which, I am sure, confused some people.

It also meant that there was no way anyone would be able to do a 'double' and win both the PDC and BDO titles in the same year – not that the BDO would have let any of us anywhere near their venue in the first place. Happily for me, 1998 turned out to be my best year with the PDC. I won my group, which featured Graeme Stoddart and Mick Manning (we all won one and lost one, but I had the best record overall so went through) before playing Harry Robinson in the quarter-finals. That was a fairly straightforward 4-1 win which meant I was in my first semi-final since I'd won the competition in 1983. That felt good. But could I go all the way and win it again, 15 years on?

My opponent in the last four was Dennis Priestley, who was one of the favourites and someone I was now looking to beat, even, if I am completely honest with you again, I was beginning to feel as if I was past my competitive best at this stage. On the morning of the semi I woke up and I felt absolutely awful; I couldn't eat or drink anything at all. It wasn't nerves either, as I'd been playing really well, despite pretty much writing myself off as a major contender beforehand. I managed to get to the venue but, even then, as I was practising, I couldn't even throw a dart and, by now was probably dehydrated as well, with Eric Bristow looking out for me and trying to get me to get some liquid on board. It was all a bit hopeless and, although I walked on to the stage and tried to look the part, there was no way I was going to beat Dennis and he comfortably won 5-1.

I couldn't even then slip away home and fall into my bed for a few days as, the next day, I was expected to play Rod Harrington in a third/fourth place play-off, a bit of a pointless exercise, as both losing semi-finalists got £3,500 prize money anyway so I offered Rod the match but it was on television and the whole point of the PDC was to get us and the events back on TV, so it wouldn't have been right for me to step away from that. Even so, I still felt lousy and didn't really give Rod a game at all and he won 4-1. Yet, despite that (and despite still feeling as if I had a dose of the man flu) I headed home, content with the few days I'd had and extremely happy that I was now back in the world rankings at number seven, something which would give me a bit of a boost for the tournaments that were still to come that year.

One of those was the World Matchplay, held, once again, in Blackpool from 27 July to 1 August. After beating Peter Evison 8-4 in the first round and Mick Manning 8-6 in the second, I came up against Peter Manley, who was seeded four, in the quarter-finals. Form and seedings, therefore, suggested Peter would beat me, especially as I was unseeded, and make his way to the semi-finals.

But I was playing some great darts by now and, even if I wasn't always hitting the big scores (in my first two matches and then my quarter-final, my three-dart averages were lower than my opponent's), I was very consistent and rarely missing what

I needed to get – something which would have meant whoever was doing the spotting in my absence would have been happy, as I'd have been making them look good. I beat Peter 13-9 which meant I was going to play the then world number one Rod Harrington in the semis.

Playing Rod at any time was a challenge and, even though I'd competed very well indeed to get this far, I knew winning against him, especially in the semi-final of a big tournament, was going to be a very tall order indeed. But I hung on in there and, after the first 16 legs, we were dead level at 8-8. So I was pleased to be doing well even though, to be fair, I was just about keeping up. I had some spare darts with me at Blackpool, which were six grams lighter than my usual darts. Every time I practised with them, I played brilliantly and couldn't miss a thing. Maybe they'd come in useful, at least that's what I thought at the time. So, before the match started, I had a quick word with Rory Hopkins, who was the producer with Sky Sports, asking him to hold on to a set of those lighter darts for me and telling him that, if I wanted them, I'd go to the camera during a break and ask him to bring them over. Which is exactly what I did at 8-8, a tactical masterstroke at exactly the right moment: at least, that is what I'd hoped. I won the very next leg in 13 darts and, as I walked up for the start of the 18th leg, I couldn't help thinking, 'What a great decision *that* was.' It hadn't worked and, although I kept Rod just about in sight from there on in, that was pretty much it, and he went on to win 13-10 before beating Ronnie Baxter 19-17 in the final.

But I wasn't complaining and, at least this time, Kim didn't have to put up with me moaning and groaning as we headed home again. For each of the two major tournaments that had been played that year, I'd reached the semi-finals, something that I truly hadn't thought I'd ever do again a few years earlier.

Playing in the big tournaments and doing well, plus, of course, all the television exposure that went with it again, was fabulous. Darts felt as if it had been reborn and, although the BDO carried on with its own events alongside the PDC, we had the very great majority of the big-name players within our ranks as well as the biggest competitions. It meant, of course, that taking part in those 'bread and butter' events, as Eric Bristow so sagely described them, was, again, going to be a major part of my working life. And, with the game in as good a place commercially as it had ever been, my sights were now set at a very high level. So, along with Eric and our families, I decided to push for a darts promotion on the *QE2*. Cunard loved the idea and, before long, we were heading off to Bermuda on what was then the most famous ship in the world. But something was missing; we needed, as I said to Eric, a catchphrase, something people would use that would immediately relate to us and the darts we'd be playing on the ship for the duration.

'Bloody marvellous,' was how I concluded that particular conversation.

And that was it. 'Bloody marvellous' it was. It caught on very quickly indeed and, by the end of the cruise, everyone on the ship was saying it to one another – and it's not really the sort of expression you expected to hear on the *QE2*. It even caught on with one of the famous people who just happened to be on the same cruise, someone who was even more well known than Eric Bristow was at the time. The man in question was the actor Gene Hackman, who'd boarded at New York and was taking the *QE2* back to Southampton. The ship's officers ended up inviting Gene to accompany them plus Eric and myself for a game of darts and, even though Gene didn't step up to throw any himself, he stayed to watch.

He wasn't the only famous face who joined in with us though, as the novelist and screenwriter Richard P. Henrick (*Crimson Tide* is one of his most well-known books) also came along, so Eric and I were pulling in the stars. It was all great fun, as much fun I guess as you can have when you are working, and, in all, I enjoyed ten years of that mix of fun and work on the *QE2* before she was 'retired'. I now live very near to Lucy, the widow of one of the ship's former captains, the late David Perkins. Lucy is a very good friend of ours, as her husband had been.

One of the numerous experiences I have enjoyed on the *QE2* was the opportunity to play the part of James Bond, giving me an idea of what life might have been like for 007. The first time came as we were making our way through the Panama Canal. Or would have been, as we got entangled in the nautical equivalent of a traffic jam, which means it took a lot longer than anyone had expected for us to get through. This meant that the ship would now not, after all, be able to sail into Cartagena, which wasn't ideal as Kim and I were due to disembark there and head back to the UK.

Cunard soon came up with a solution. The captain slowed the ship right down and, as he did so, the cruise director came up to me, saying, 'Mr Deller, you have one hour to get all of your things packed,' before he turned to Kim and added, 'Please do not wear a dress, Mrs Deller, as you will be climbing down a rope ladder.' Kim thought he was joking but no, off we went, departing the *QE2* and down into a small boat sailing alongside her which took us away from the ship and off to Panama City for us to fly home.

But, as if those adventures on the high seas weren't enough, I then had another adventure at sea, this time when I was working on *Ocean Village*. I was due to pick up the ship in Antigua and was supposed to be flying out there from Heathrow but that flight was cancelled, so I was quickly put in a taxi and sent off to Gatwick. This meant I still arrived, as expected, in Antigua, but three-quarters of an hour after the ship had left, as *Ocean Village* would have been fined a lot of money if she had stayed in dock for longer than she should have done. So on this occasion, special agent Deller was put on a speedboat which rushed out to *Ocean Village*, and had around 1,000 spectators on hand to watch him get on board via yet another rope ladder. And no, I wasn't wearing a dress.

Working on P&O Ferries, on the other hand, could never be as grand as doing so on the *QE2* or *Ocean Village*. Yet, for all that, I spent many happy years doing exhibitions on the

Hull to Rotterdam crossing. They were very popular and we'd usually take 800 happy customers with us on a two-day trip. It was a party atmosphere from beginning to end, although the price of drinks on the ferry was so low, which was probably a major contributing factor to the general bonhomie on board. I'd work P&O with Phil Taylor, Raymond van Barneveld and Gary Anderson, all of whom seemed to enjoy it as much as I did. Then, for the last three years I worked with them, my good friend and former world number one Colin Lloyd came along and we'd pair up together. But, as enjoyable as it all was for both Kim and me, you just couldn't beat the cruise ships. The *QE2* was beyond special, as were the ships operated by Fred Olsen and, for the last ten years of my working life, those belonging to Royal Caribbean. They were special trips and wonderful memories as a result of promotions that opened up for me, and still do, because of my World Championship win back in 1983.

That 138 really did change my life and in ways that, even now, I look back on and still find more than a little unbelievable.

9

Characters

You couldn't argue with Eric

MY BEST mate in darts is Mr Glitter himself, the one and only Bobby George. I first met Bobby when I was 13 and, straight away, Bobby referred to me as 'the boy'.

I'm 61 now and he still calls me as 'the boy'. But I'm not complaining, not now anyway. He'd often call around to my parents' house when I was still living there. On one occasion, when I was about 21, we'd arranged for me to drive him to a tournament in Norwich. He came round to the house as usual and, when he arrived, he asked Mum if she'd iron his trousers for him? 'Of course I will Bobby,' she replied. 'Where are they?' With that, Bobby took the pair he was wearing off, gave them to her and sat down on the sofa in just his pants. I was beyond embarrassed but couldn't help laughing out loud at the same time. You just had to take Bobby as he came and that was part of him.

He was, and remains, a great friend. Some years back, when we were in Los Angeles, some of his friends out there told him they were taking a boat out to go shark fishing. Bobby loved his fishing, so he said he'd come along. I also thought it might be an interesting trip, so I agreed to join them. Did I enjoy it? If feeling like death and spending the first four hours of the trip down below feeling seasick was 'enjoying' the trip, then yes, I did. I got over the seasickness eventually though and was soon feeling well enough to have a beer, so I went up on to the deck and asked Bobby if they'd caught anything yet. They hadn't, so I asked if I could take over and sat down in his place, with the rod.

After about half an hour or so, the rod moved, so I reeled it in. Once I'd got it back, I pointed to what was on the end of the hook and said to Bobby, 'Look at this, I've caught loads of fish.' But Bobby wasn't so impressed.

'You idiot, that's the bait for my shark.'

That was the end of my fishing days.

On another occasion, Bobby and I were in Scotland along with Eric Bristow. We'd finished the exhibition we'd been booked to do and, after a few drinks, Eric and Bobby suggested that we got some curries in, as they were particularly partial to them. Eric took his up to his room while, as Bobby's room had two twin beds in it, we both took ours there. It was quite dark in his room, so much so that I didn't realise, as I was eating mine, that half of it was going into my mouth as intended but the other half was going all over the bed and the floor.

We'd all agreed to meet the next morning for breakfast at 9am before leaving at 9.45 for the next show. But by departure time, there was still no sign of Bobby, so I went up to his room thinking that he'd overslept. To my surprise I found him down on his hands and knees scrubbing the floor. I'm not going to repeat what he said to me here, but, needless to say, we did all have a laugh about it later on that day.

In 1979 I travelled to the States with Bobby. I still wasn't quite 21 at the time and a little bit naïve still in some of the ways of the world, so Bobby was a perfect travelling companion to have. One of the events we were down to play in was an open tournament at a venue called Chris's Bar in Vallejo, California.

The only problem was that, as I still wasn't 21, I wasn't allowed into the bar. That meant that even though I was supposed to be a member of our team, I had to spend five hours sat outside in a van along with some local teenagers. Oh the glamour. Mind you, Bobby did look after me, making sure that I had a bottle of Coke, a straw and a packet of crisps (or chips, as they call them out there) for company as I sat that particular event out.

Bobby brought an element of showbiz to our sport that people love, and even today they enjoy seeing him at tournaments and exhibitions for that very reason. His walk-on, together with his candelabra and cloak, is pure theatre and long may it continue.

Big Cliff Lazarenko was also a great friend, someone who always went out of his way to look after me. Cliff was very much a people person and, in a way, reminded me of the character

Norm from the TV programme *Cheers*. We shared many laughs but, even so, whenever we were out and having a laugh together, I had to pace my drinking with Cliff as he never changed. His favourite drink was always Strongbow; he could knock as many as 25 pints of that back and still look as if he'd had just the one.

Cliff was once drawn to play against Steve Beaton in the World Matchplay in an afternoon match. To prepare, Cliff put in some serious training, starting with ten pints at the Duke of York pub before having another five at the Winter Gardens. He then strolled into the venue and beat Steve before saying, 'Let's all go out now and have a proper drink.' That was Cliff, a people's champion if ever there was one, who'd enjoy nothing more than a seat at the bar so he could chat to anyone and everyone who was there, just like Norm.

Cliff and I would often end up playing on the *QE2* together. We were such good mates that it was really hard for both of us when we had to play one another but, win or lose, we'd shake hands at the end of the exhibition and go off, along with Kim and Carol, his wife, for a meal and a few drinks. On another occasion, Cliff and I were playing in a tournament in Chicago. It started at 10am but, for some reason, the bar didn't open for another hour. As far as Cliff and I were concerned, this was nothing short of a disaster. Cliff then came up to me and said he'd noticed some locals having a good time a few doors up from where our hotel rooms were, so we went to look at what they were getting up to and gatecrashed their party. It seemed a bit of a strange one to me though as, despite it being very much an adults only affair, the only food I could see on offer was jelly which, to me, was not only the sort of thing you saw at children's parties but was not really an appropriate item for breakfast as it was, at the time, about 8am.

One of the guys at the party then told me to try one of them, so I picked up and ate what turned out to be a strawberry-flavoured jelly.

Talk about a wolf in sheep's clothing. That innocent-looking tree ended up blowing my mind. It was filled with vodka and, after an hour or so and a few more portions, Cliff and I came out of the room in very high spirits indeed. I don't know exactly how many he'd had, but I thought I'd downed at least eight double vodkas and boy, was I ready to play in this tournament now.

I also enjoy going out with Colin Lloyd and we've become good friends over the years. Colin is a top man and an exceptional darts player who has become one of the most successful to date with the PDC.

Russ Bray is, perhaps, someone who is better known for his voice than his face. Russ is one of the best referees as well as a caller, a very distinctive one at that as well. He's a good friend in darts as well as away from the game. We've been working together now for the same company for 16 years or so and do a lot of corporate shows together. We also socialise with our wives and often pop down to London to see some of the shows together. I'm due to play in the World Seniors Championship in February 2022 and, when I do, Russ is going to be my wingman.

What can I say about Eric Bristow? When he started working for Sky, we became really close friends and would speak nearly every day of the year, including on my birthday, Christmas Eve and Christmas Day. Eric had a reputation of being the showman and even a bit cocky with it, but he had a softer side to his character that the general public never saw. If, for example, we'd been away at an exhibition, he would always remind me to text him when I got home, so he knew I was back and safe.

People say, even today, that Eric had a touch of arrogance about him. My response to that is to say a lot of the world's greatest sports stars might come across that way, but it isn't necessarily arrogance, even though that might seem the case. I think Eric had an aura about him, just as another Eric, Eric Cantona, whenever he played football. Cantona would strut about the pitch as if he owned it; sometimes he had this look of disdain on his face which spoke of how he couldn't quite believe he was there and that everyone watching should be honoured to be in his presence.

I think our darting great Eric was a bit like that. On his day, he was so brilliant that you knew it was unlikely you'd get anywhere near him. He didn't come on to the stage hoping to win, or wanting people to wish him luck; he'd feel it was pre-ordained that he would win, such would be his confidence in his ability. That is why, I think, people misinterpreted that as arrogance. He was a darts genius, it was as simple as that. We'd be in the practice room before a big tournament started and Eric would walk in, eyeball the trophy and tell everyone in earshot, whether they wanted to listen to him or not, that he'd already made room in his car for it. It really used to bug us when he arrived and started giving it out like that and Jocky Wilson would, in particular, usually bite back – but then that is exactly what Eric would have wanted.

On one occasion, at the Dry Blackthorn Cider Masters, we were all in the practice room and were asked by the organisers to say what we all thought of Eric. This was an elite event as all of the top eight players in the world at the time were there, so they were clearly hoping for, shall we say, some 'interesting' material. I didn't really want any part of what they were doing, so when I was called up to say a few words about Eric, I kept it simple, saying he was the best player in the world and just being diplomatic. Job done. Bobby George, on the other hand, claimed that Eric was a 'cry baby' and, when he lost a match, he'd 'run to his mummy'. That probably wasn't Bobby's best moment. He was playing Eric in the first round and Eric just said, 'Keep the film running as I will beat him 3-0.' And he did.

John Lowe, on the other hand, wanted no part of it. And he couldn't be dissuaded. So they moved on to Jocky Wilson who, at the time, was not getting on very well with Eric and was more than happy to have his say. So, when the interviewer asked Jocky, then the world number two, what he thought of Eric, Jocky answered, 'He is the best player in the world – but he is also a ****.' Naturally enough, that response shocked the interviewer who quickly said, 'You can't say that word,

Jocky.' So Jocky apologised and they ran the camera again for a second take.

'Jocky Wilson, world number two, what do you think of Eric Bristow?'

'What do I think of Eric Bristow? Well, he is a great player and he is a great champion. But he's still a ****.'

Everyone in the room was falling about laughing by now but, sadly, the footage recorded was never used.

Eric was a master at winding people up and, when he did, Jocky usually felt the brunt of it.

Jocky's large and boisterous fan base, much like their man, didn't like Eric either. On one particularly memorable occasion, England were playing Scotland up in Edinburgh and were winning easily. But that didn't really matter to the 3,000 or so Scottish spectators, who were only interested in the outcome of one match – Jocky Wilson versus Eric Bristow. The atmosphere didn't faze Eric one little bit and he beat Jocky 3-0 before saluting the crowd, something which didn't go down particularly well. Once the match had ended and the England players were all brought up on to the stage, Bobby George came up first, then Eric, who would be followed by yours truly.

But before I even got on to the edge of the stage, beer cans were being thrown on to it and all I could see in the melee was Bobby ducking down out of the way and the TV cameras being smashed up, which was the cue for the BBC to make an announcement to the effect that, due to circumstances out of its control, its wouldn't now be televising the presentation.

I usually got in and out of tournaments and exhibitions in Scotland without any trouble, primarily, I think, because I got on well with Jocky and the respect and friendship between us hadn't been lost on his fan base. Wales, however, was a different matter. I'd had problems there in the past (see Chapter Five) and, a couple of years later, I was heading back there for an international. I was a bit worried about how my presence back there would go down with the Welsh supporters, so had a quick word to that effect with Eric, telling him I was worried about my safety.

'Leave it to me,' said Eric.

He knew someone who'd not long been out of prison who would be able to get me to and from the venue quickly and in complete safety. So, after the match was finished, I was out and in this chap's car, ready to get back to the safety of my hotel only for one of the Wales fans to see me.

'There's Deller!' he shouted at his mates. That was enough for my newly appointed driver to take action, so he promptly sped towards the fan in the car and just, in passing, caught him on his leg. I was immediately worried about him and said so, but Eric's mate just said, 'I only clipped him,' and got me back to my hotel in double quick time.

I got in and called Eric, telling him what had happened.

'Keith, did he get you back all right and in one piece?'

'Yes Eric, but...'

'Well he did his job then, didn't he?'

You couldn't argue with Eric.

I was back in Wales a short time afterwards, playing in the Welsh Open. I'd got through to the last 32, which was quite an achievement for me considering that every time I threw my darts, some bloke in the audience who was sat right behind me was giving me the worst kind of verbal abuse you can imagine. I turned round at one point to look at him, only for him to emphasise how he wanted to put his hands around my throat – and squeeze. Back then, when things could get a little bit lively, Eric would take five lads with him whose brief was, essentially, to look after him and keep him safe. Once we'd finished, Eric, along with his, let's say 'staff', came up to me and said, 'When you're ready to go, me and the boys will take you and Kim to your car.' That didn't take long as I lost my next match, meaning it was time for Kim and I to leave. The same bloke was waiting for me outside again, so Eric looked him in the eye and said, 'Don't even think about it.' We got in the car safely and, as we were leaving, I asked Kim to pull up where this chap still was, wound down the window and said to him 'And as for you!' before giving him the V sign.

Eric later said to me, 'If you'd have stalled at that point, you'd have been on your own.'

When he died in 2018, I was at the Premier League event in Liverpool and was asked by the producer how I'd feel about going up on to the stage with Dave Clark, the presenter. I did, but it was one of the hardest things that I've ever had to do. The crowd, though, were very understanding and supportive and helped me along the way and I was so pleased, ultimately, to be able to speak about a friend who I still miss to this day. He will, for me, always be the biggest name the sport has ever had and I can say with absolute confidence that if it hadn't been for Eric Bristow, darts would be nowhere near the level it is at today.

I had a long and very competitive rivalry with Jocky Wilson even before I became the world champion in 1983 – he'd had the courtesy, if you remember, to speak well of me at those championships, saying that even though I was an 'unknown' to a lot of people, I was, as far as the people within the game were concerned, a very good player who had already earned their respect. He didn't have to say that, especially after I'd just knocked him out, and I was very appreciative of his words and respect at that time.

On one of my trips to the USA to play in a tournament there, Jocky was joining me along with Cliff Lazarenko. Cliff was a former builder so he asked three of his mates from the sites to join him on the trip. They all met at the airport bar and, as you'd expect, drank a toast to the success of going Stateside. We all had a few pints and, before we knew it, all six of us were on the plane and heading off across the pond.

After about an hour or so, the drinks came around as well as a few packets of peanuts. One of Cliff's mates quickly ate all of his peanuts before asking Cliff when the in-flight meal would be served as he was getting hungry.

'Not for another hour or so,' replied Cliff, who was well used to how these things worked on long flights – serve the peanuts, get the punters thirsty so they'll drink more. Rinse and repeat.

'Well are there any more peanuts then?'

Cliff knew that Jocky liked peanuts, but he also knew that Jocky would just suck the salt from them before putting the peanuts back into the packet. So Cliff turned to Jocky and asked him if he wanted his peanuts.

'No, your mate can have them,' replied Jocky.

Cliff gave the packet to his mate who put it up to his mouth, tipping the whole of the contents inside, before saying, in between chews, 'There's no salt on these ones.'

Cliff looked at his mate, then at Jocky, before replying, 'Look at Jocky.'

Jocky was sat there with a big smile on his face, with all the salt from the peanuts smeared around his lips, which was the cue for Cliff's mate to make a very swift exit to the plane's toilet.

On another occasion, I was in Belgium and sharing a cabin with Jocky and the Canadian player John Part. The tournament that we'd been playing in was over and Jocky had decided to head out to a club with some of the locals. We had to be up at 5am the next day in order to have enough time to make the airport and our flights home but Jocky, having had his night out, was back at 4am, meaning he had only an hour to get some sleep before he was off again. We all got up on time but found that Jocky had fallen asleep with half of his body wedged into the fridge in his room and an opened can of beer on the floor next to him. We all made a tremendous effort to get him out and away on time and on to the minibus that was taking us to the airport. Once we were there and through the gates, ready to make for our respective flights, we reminded Jocky not to miss his, but he fell asleep and ended up staying for another day in Belgium.

Jocky would often be the butt of other people's jokes, but he always took it well. Eric was playing in a match against him up in Scotland where, as you'd expect, the atmosphere was extremely lively, especially as Eric was winning. This clearly irked someone in the crowd who decided to throw a couple of cans of beer at Eric on the stage. They missed him but hit the playing area, prompting Eric to take the microphone and loudly announce to all the partisan Scots in the audience, 'Whoever threw those is just like Jocky, you can't hit anything either.'

Typical Eric, he had a ready comment for just about any occasion.

Another incident involving Jocky took place at a British Open. I'd been playing on board four, while Jocky was next door to me on board five. This meant we were due to play one another in the last 32. I was at the table by our board when this chap, who was wearing glasses, came up to Jocky and said to him, and I'm toning down the language here, something to the effect that he was a 'horrible little Scotsman'. Except it was a lot stronger than that. Jocky promptly took the fella's glasses off before punching him to the ground, then turning round and saying, 'You never hit someone with their glasses on. Now, what board am I on?' only for an official, who'd witnessed the whole thing, to reply, 'You've just knocked your opponent out, so you are disqualified.'

That certainly made my part of the draw a little bit easier.

Eric also played against Jocky when he was a member of the England team taking on a Rest of the World side which Jocky was part of, an event that was big enough to be broadcast on ITV immediately after *News At Ten*. Jocky, who was captain of the Rest of the World side, played every member of the English team (everyone played each other in one leg of 501) and promptly lost to all of them, meaning that, in the end, the English team won easily. Once the match was over, both teams lined up for the presentations and, as they did, Jocky turned to Eric and said, 'I'm a proud man to be captain of the Rest of the World,' to which Eric replied, 'It's a shame that you didn't play like it then.'

Once the presentations were over, the officials had to pull Jocky off Eric, who knew exactly how to wind you up and he'd certainly done so again with Jocky that day. If ever a man wasn't going to be lost for words, it was Eric Bristow. We both played in the Samson Classic, which used to be shown on Tyne-Tees, and one year was won by Eric. It was a funny trophy as well; imagine something like the FA Cup, only what it would look like if it had been cut in half. Eric took one look at it during the presentation and said, 'I'll make sure I come back next year, so I can win the other half of this,' which he did, although he just got to keep the same 'half trophy' for another year.

I used to particularly enjoy playing doubles with Eric. We'd teamed up for a tournament in Chicago one year to play cricket, the name of the most popular darts game in the USA. The objective is to get three of a particular number but scoring only if you managed to do that and your opponents didn't while working downwards from 20 through to 15 and the bullseye. All we needed to win was 25, the outer ring of the bullseye. I'd done most of the work and, even though we hadn't yet won the match and I was standing right next to our two opponents, Eric turned to me and said I'd asked one of them to go to the control table to see who we'd be playing in the semi-final before stepping up and getting the 25 that we needed. That was that, a bit of psychological warfare from Eric of course, but there you go. Anyway, we all shook hands and, as we did so, one of them said to me, 'Keith, you're a real nice guy, but Eric, well, that guy is one helluva asshole.'

That was playing with Eric all over – it could be eventful, but it was always fun.

One of the great characters of the game for me was Leighton Rees. Leighton was a former world number one as well as the first winner of the BDO World Championship in 1978, beating John Lowe in the final. He was also a really nice guy, great company to be in and a man who always had a smile on his face. I have very happy memories of playing him in the first round of the British Matchplay one year when it was being held at a holiday camp in Great Yarmouth with the Anglia TV cameras in attendance. It was a lively affair, not least because of the presence of Paul and Oliver Croft, the sons of Olly Croft who ran the BDO. Paul and Oliver liked to party and it wasn't unknown for as many as 40 people to be packed into their caravan partying the night away on site while the tournament was being played.

I was at one of their parties one night. It was close to one in the morning and their caravan was just two away from where Leighton was staying. He was due to be playing against me later on that day with a 10.40am start but, like me, he was out late as well. Someone therefore thought, in Leighton's absence, that it might be a good idea to throw a few loaves of bread on to the roof of his caravan.

Everyone went to bed eventually, even Leighton, but he wouldn't have been asleep for long for, at dawn, the hundreds of seagulls that roosted in and around the park were up for breakfast and, much to their delight, they soon noticed that a buffet had been laid on for them on Leighton's roof. They descended upon it in numbers and the noise and general commotion was so loud that Leighton, desperately trying to get some sleep, must have thought the roof was about to cave in. The disturbance certainly didn't put him in a very good frame of mind, especially as he was down to play me in just a few hours' time. He promptly sought me out in the practice room later that morning and asked me if I knew anything about what had happened and, with as straight a face as I could manage, I said, 'No, Leighton,' realising, at the same time, I owed Paul and Oliver a few beers, especially as I won the match 3-0.

Another good story that features Leighton was at the British Open one year, a tournament that anyone could enter so, feasibly, you could be a pub player who ended up competing against one of the big names in the game. It was certainly an attractive enough event to get covered by ITV, so there'd be a big enough home audience for some of the matches to tempt the 1,500 or so players who'd enter it every year.

Big Cliff Lazarenko was there as usual, my best friend on the circuit and a man who liked to warm up with perhaps a dozen or so cans of Strongbow before his matches started. On this occasion, Cliff was in action at 10am while Leighton was playing in the second of the two daily sessions, which started at 2pm. Cliff noticed that Leighton was there so asked him if he had any beers in his kitbag, to which Leighton, generous to a fault, said that he had, and that Cliff was welcome to help himself. This arrangement suited Cliff down to the ground as the bar wasn't due to open for another couple of hours, so he took Leighton up on his kind offer and helped himself to all the cans that were in there, drinking them one by one until there weren't any left. Later on that day, and with his match about to start, Leighton thought he'd have a couple of beers to get himself warmed up only to find out that Cliff hadn't even left one for him to have.

You'd think that would at least have sent Leighton into his match with a clear head, but it didn't do him any good as Cliff went on to win the tournament, assisted, no doubt, by the good start he'd had courtesy of Leighton's largesse.

We were all taking part in an event in Ireland a couple of months later and, prior to the day's matches starting, I was sat in a hotel room with Cliff and John Lowe when there was a knock on the door. It was Leighton.

'Mr Lazarenko,' he said, 'I am drinking 20 cans of beer before I leave this room.' And to be fair to Leighton, he gave it a good go.

That was what the darts was like back in the day. We all prepared for our matches together and we certainly all drank together but, when it came to playing the matches, all we wanted to do was beat our opponent, no matter who it was, or how much of a mate he might have been. The friendships we all made were great ones that still last today but the rivalries were even greater and, once you were up on that stage, you didn't have a mate up there with you, just an opponent. Yet, once the match was over and we'd shaken hands and either congratulated our opponent or commiserated with him, that intensity was gone and we'd be looking to go out and have a meal together somewhere.

Some people just didn't get on though. Eric Bristow, for example, didn't like Alan Evans and it used to show, especially in some of their early matches. It might have been because, while Eric liked to play quickly and get the game over and done with, Alan's style of play was a little more slow and deliberate; an approach or tactic, call it whatever you want, that may well have put Eric off, and it wasn't unknown for any animosity between the two of them to occasionally show in their matches. Mind you, it didn't do the game or the publicity surrounding either player any harm. The sparks that you know are going to fly in matches like that cause a great deal of interest and everyone wants to see them.

There is always going to be a lot of testosterone around when a load of blokes are together, especially if it is in a competitive environment. Everyone wants to win, no matter what you are doing – and it needn't always be on the stage, as that inbuilt desire to prove that you are top dog remains all the time. Once, when we were all playing in the Berlin Open, the temperature outside the venue was -23°C. In addition to that, the snow that had blanketed the place was now at least two feet deep, with the threat of more to come. Phil Taylor had, as usual, won the event so, not long afterwards, a few of us thought it would only be right and proper if we were to offer him our congratulations, albeit with snowballs.

So, the moment Phil walked outside, someone shouted 'Fire!' and Phil found himself absolutely bombarded by a constant stream of shots. He was up for it though, as he carefully put his trophy down before chasing after us, eventually ending up rolling over and over in the snow with Rod Harrington. Phil gave as good as he got, but he'd been wiped out by the sheer number of snowballs thrown at him, all of which hit the target – but even that gave him some ammunition of his own as he fired back, and typically had the last word, 'It's a shame that you were all not so accurate on the dartboard.'

One of the funniest things I was ever involved with took place when I was invited to appear in a Christmas Day edition of *Bullseye*, ITV's darts-based quiz show hosted by the late Jim Bowen. It was scheduled to start at about 3.10pm, so straight after the Queen's speech. That meant it had a captive audience and I understand that around 21 million people watched it that year, a phenomenal number of viewers, even for back then.

The three darts players in attendance were myself, Eric Bristow and Jocky Wilson. As it was the Christmas show, we were all asked to dress up, so Eric came along as a Pearly King, Jocky was in formal Scottish dress and I was dressed as a schoolboy. In addition to us, there were a couple of celebrity guests, Rod Hull and Emu. Rod was well known for using Emu as a platform for attacking whatever celebrities he happened to be with, the BBC chat show host Michael Parkinson having been one of his most famous victims – although Rod would always deny responsibility and say that it was all down to Emu, not him. Nevertheless, the presence of Emu used to make people nervous, not so much of being 'attacked' but that, when – rather than if – they were, it did all look a bit humiliating for people to see you being wrestled to the ground by an oversized puppet, something that was most certainly not good for your reputation.

Eric knew this and, when Rod and Emu came to say hello to us before the show, Eric said to Rod, 'If you come anywhere near me with that emu, I will knock you out.' So Rod knew where he stood with Eric. There'd be no repeat of what had happened with Parky. Jocky then sidled up to Rod, took his sgian-dubh (the small, single-edged knife worn as part of the traditional Highland dress) and showed it to Emu before saying, 'Come near me and I will cut the emu.'

So Rod and Emu now knew exactly where they stood with Eric and Jocky. I guess that meant Emu had his eye on me but

240

nothing of note happened and we all got to the end of the show relatively unscathed – even Jocky, who was on edge throughout as Eric had told him that, after what he'd said to Rod, 'The emu is going to get you.'

Jocky kept himself at more than arm's length from Emu for the rest of the show after that and, at the end, when we were all stood there waving at the camera as the credits go up, you could see Jocky looking over at Emu and mouthing a few choice words to him – with so much intent that I told Eric he really should let Jocky know that he was winding him up. He never did though.

I was often asked to appear on *Bullseye* and fondly remember another appearance, this time without Emu. The show was filmed in Birmingham and they always recorded two episodes in the one day, back to back. On the day before ours, Eric Bristow had been on along with Maureen Flowers, who was the number one-ranked female player for much of the 1980s. Once they'd finished recording, they both, as you always did in those days, made for the hotel bar where they were staying in order to have a few drinks with some of the TV people. Eric was sat at the bar with his drink as someone started playing on the piano, so, quick as a flash, Eric shouted out that the player '...sounded like Stevie Wonder'. That's because the player in question was Stevie Wonder, who'd just done a show at the nearby NEC and was appearing there again the following night, which was when I'd be in there with Kim.

We made sure we got to that bar after my show the following day, all set to be entertained by an impromptu show by Stevie, but, sadly, he didn't show up that time, although we did notice Penelope Keith and Roger Cook, the TV 'investigator', at breakfast the next morning.

I wonder if they'll mention in any books they go on to write about their lives that they once shared a hotel breakfast with that darts player, Keith whatsisname?

I never did *Bullseye* with Phil Taylor. But if I had done, he'd have practised beforehand. And on that board they use for the show. He'd have wanted to win and he would have expected his playing partner, even if they just played the game for fun in their local on a Friday night, to have the same mentality.

I think that, as far as Phil is concerned, I should just say 'The Greatest', and leave it at that. Because he is, for me, the greatest darts player of all time. No contest. I'm also very proud to say he is a very good friend. But what is it about Phil that sets him apart from everyone else?

I'll tell you. It's not so much about his physical game as what is in his mind. Phil's mindset is completely different to everyone else's in the game. He'd be there on a Sunday night, holding the winner's trophy and a big cheque after another big tournament win, with the Sky cameras on him and while being interviewed on the stage with thousands of people cheering him and singing his name.

But for all of that, at 9am the following day, Phil would be back on the practice board and putting in the hours as he planned his next big win. That's the side of winners you don't see, the time spent practising, hour after hour after hour, day in and day out. Practice, practice, practice. And then some. That is the Phil Taylor away from the TV cameras, the very definition of being a professional sportsperson. Yes, he enjoys the moment of triumph. But its only fleeting for, as soon as he had tasted it, he wanted to do so again.

Wherever he would go and whatever tournament he was playing in, Phil wanted to win. I've already mentioned how, after he'd won the Berlin Open, we all offered him our congratulations by throwing snowballs at him. Phil took that in the sort of good spirit you'd expect.

And yes, it was 'only' the Berlin Open. But he'd have taken it as seriously as the World Championship. He just wants to win at everything he does. Even though he was completely outnumbered by all of us with the snowballs, he was probably thinking of ways he could overcome us at that, even though the odds were against him. It's what he does. Mind you, one of the people he didn't catch up with in all that snow was me as I was too quick for him.

He'd come up to me at all the televised tournaments when we were playing in the same session, and always saying the same thing. He even made up some shirts for me, which I thought was a nice touch. They had the same phrase that he kept saying to me woven on the back. Dynamite Deller.

Every time. Without fail. I didn't mind; in fact I was quite flattered about it to be honest and said to him after he'd done it yet again, 'Why do you call me "Dynamite", Phil, is it because of my explosive play?'

'No,' Phil replied. 'It's because you always blow up in the early rounds.'

The cheeky devil.

On another occasion, I was playing him in the last 16 of the Eastbourne Open. There were 200 people packed into the venue and I was able to put on a show for them, beating him. At that event, the losers had to score the next match. Mine was against Robbie Widdows, and, with respect to Robbie, I should have won, especially as I'd just come off a big win over Phil.

'Come on loser,' I said to Phil. 'Get them chalks.'

What happened? Robbie threw a big finish to win while I was sitting on a double. Phil just looked at me and said, 'Come on, loser,' and we went out for a meal.

Phil Taylor. The ultimate professional. But also a complete and utter gentleman.

If you could describe anyone in darts as the pro's pro then John Lowe would get my vote, and no doubt a lot of the other players' votes too, every single time. Everything John does reflects his professionalism. He pays attention to every little minor detail and was probably aware of, and applying, the philosophy of 'marginal gains'[3] long before it became a stock phrase. He is always immaculately dressed and, if you were ever going to coach or copy someone's throw, then it would be John's. He had a close group of friends in the game, including big Cliff, and it was through John's friendship with him that I got to know Cliff.

---

3   The marginal gains theory is concerned with small incremental improvements in any process, which, when added together, make a significant improvement.

I was playing against John in the 1984 World Matchplay when he achieved the sport's first televised nine-dart finish, our equivalent of making a 147 break in snooker. From a historical point of view, it was good for me to be part of his achievement as I'll always be referred to as the unlucky bloke he was playing at the time, although it bothered me that he did it as he also proceeded to knock me out of the competition. John won £102,000 for the nine-darter, a massive prize that, I suspect, the sponsors thought no one had a realistic chance of winning, meaning their money was safe. But if anyone was going to do it then it would have been John, the man who has won three individual world titles in three different decades (1979, 1987, 1993) and whose service to the game and the charities he supports saw him deservedly awarded the MBE in 2018.

* * *

Looking back at some of the escapades we all got into never fails to put a smile on my face. We played hard, very hard, and some of us would have fought one another given half a chance. But we always, and I mean always, ensured that we had some good laughs as we did so. It's not the same in the game today and the players are all a lot more competitive and disciplined in their approach. Darts comes first, second and third for them while, on top of that, there is so much money involved in the game today that there is also a fair bit of jealousy and people end up being very careful about what they are doing and who they are seen doing it with. In addition to all of that, they also have the all-.

3seeing eye of the Darts Regulation Authority (DRA) to think about. The DRA is the game's disciplinary body and will not hesitate to come down hard on anyone it thinks is bringing the game into disrepute or damaging its reputation in any way.

10

The Spotter

'Keith, you must have a maths degree?'

A NEW millennium and, for me, a year in 2001, that could not have started better.

I'd played in the Eastbourne singles which is, even though it sounds a modest affair, a world-ranking event. I got to the final with little to no difficulty on the way and ended up winning it by beating John Part. Winning any tournament felt great but what was, for me, just as important was the fact I was now ranked number five in the world, not a bad achievement for someone who'd been involved with the game at the highest level for the best part of two decades by then.

So it's fair to say the night after my success saw me buzzing. I was in the hotel bar with my good friend and sponsor, Rab Bain, who said that, even though we were on a big high at the time, we should just play it cool. Seconds later, Peter Manley and a few of the other players who'd been at the tournament walked into the bar and Rab said, 'My round then,' before looking at me and saying, 'What do you want to drink, Champ?' Rab was a great friend and sponsor for both me and darts in general and has, over the years, spent over £500,000 sponsoring players.

A week after my win, I was on my way to see Rab in order to pick up some new shirts when my phone rang. It was Kim, who told me to pull off the road before she would speak to me.

'Keith, you have a life-threatening illness and need to get over to Addenbrooke's Hospital immediately.'

That was not the sort of call you expected or wanted, especially on a day when everything in life seemed to be falling into place for you.

Not long after I arrived at Addenbrooke's, I was in a private room with all manner of tubes stuck on and in me. It wasn't long before the national press heard about my condition and I was soon on the front of all the newspapers. A few reporters soon tracked down my brother, who told them I'd suffered from a brain haemorrhage, although that wasn't the case. What did happen was that I had an MRI scan that took an age – they're noisy things, although the technology involved with them is nothing short of miraculous, and you need to keep still for the duration – but, eventually, they slid me out and a consultant came in to see me.

'Mr Deller,' he said. 'You have an aneurysm and it's a very serious one. It is, in effect, a time bomb inside you that might go off at any moment.'

You can imagine how hearing that news brought me back down to earth very quickly after the highs of my win in Eastbourne.

I spent the next nine days in Addenbrooke's and, it's fair to say (and I am sure a lot of people will relate to this) that all the sitting around I was doing gave me a lot of thinking time.

Is my career over?

And, worse than that.

Am I going to die?

Just as all of this was happening, a big event in Northern Ireland was scheduled to start so, of course, I had Rab on the phone.

'When are you coming out, Keith? I've got a helicopter ready to get you out there.'

I'd forgotten all about the event. I ripped all the wires out, half toppled out of the bed and staggered towards the nurses' hub to tell them I was discharging myself as I had an event to play in and there was a helicopter waiting for me.

Which is, of course, precisely what I didn't do. Though I probably wished I could have done.

'Rab, I'm not going anywhere, mate.'

Thankfully, I fully recovered and was soon playing darts again but it was a frightening time for us both. Yet that wasn't the end of the darker moments that we lived through during that time. I was now well enough to travel again and had headed out to Boston, Massachusetts, to play in a tournament there. We'd just finished up and I'd gone to bed when the phone in my room rang at about 3am. I immediately thought it was one of the other players on a wind-up, but no, and how I wish it had been. It was Kim, who was ringing to tell me her mum, Sheila, had just passed away in hospital, from cancer, at the age of 57.

Far, far too young.

There was a little follow-up to all of this and it relates to the operation I had to fix my 'lazy eye' (see Chapter One) when I was five. I'd gone to see an eye specialist as when I'd had the aneurysm my eyelid had dropped, so as well as looking at the health of my right eye in general, they were also looking to do something about the eyelid. I was worried that any procedure on my eyes might have meant that I had to give up darts, as well as the spotting. I was assured though that, apart from a small risk of double vision, which could be rectified, I should be fine. So I had the operation and, although I had some double vision when I woke up, they were able to readjust my eye and everything was fine from that point onwards, which was a massive relief. The surgeon who did that operation on my eye, Mr Vivian, was also the doctor I'd seen in 2001. It was his suggestion that I had the MRI scan, which ultimately saved my life. Kim had initially noticed that the pupil in my right eye was smaller than the one in my left, which had led to that appointment and the subsequent phone call I'd had from Kim while I was on my way to see Rab Bain about those shirts. She, Mr Vivian and Dr Bell, who was the first person I saw, all combined and if it wasn't for their efforts, I probably wouldn't be here today.

I haven't, fortunately, been involved in too many controversial incidents during my time in the game and, as I eased into my 40s I reckoned that any chances I had of being the Alex 'Hurricane' Higgins of darts had well and truly passed me by. However, that was before my first-round match against Rod Harrington in the 2002 PDC World Championship. It ended up being a very tight game indeed, one that, for me, was highlighted by Rod tapping me on the back of my foot on three separate occasions just as I was about to throw my last dart. To me, it felt as if Rod, who was seeded at three, was feeling the pressure a bit, hence his actions and I thought this was a bit of a dirty tactic on his part. Rod, on the other hand, and this was brought up in the commentary by Sid Waddell and John Gwynne, thought I was taking too long to make my shots and his actions had been borne out of frustration. It ended up being, for me, a moot point in the end, as Rod went on to win 4-3 but we still ended up having words with one another backstage afterwards.

The whole thing turned into a watershed moment for darts, though, as following our 'confrontation' the PDC brought in the exclusion zone rule, the area of the stage that a player is not permitted to enter while his opponent is playing. It was all, perhaps, a sign of just how much pressure all of the players were under by then, and an incident that probably would never have happened 20 or even just ten years earlier.

Rod and I have always been good friends, despite that, although it did take him about 15 years to admit that he was deliberately giving me a tap on the back of my foot back then.

By 2007, I'd been playing for nearly a quarter of a century and felt that it was time to retire from competitive darts. I had to be completely honest with myself: I was no longer good enough to win the big events and did not, as a result of this, want to become the player who everyone else fancied getting in the early stages of a draw. I was during my career one of only three players, alongside Eric Bristow and Jocky Wilson, to win the top two tournaments, the World Championship and the British Professional Championship. I'd also got to the final of the World Masters and, had I won that, I would have achieved the triple crown, which only Eric had so far managed to do.

I still got the buzz from competition though, as I was enjoying my work with Sky Sports. I loved being at all the great arenas of the game and watching some of the newer players on the scene taking darts to another level. Sky has completely revolutionised darts and its coverage, and all for the better. The broadcasts feature 32 cameras at the World Championship but Sky is never resting on its already considerable laurels as it is always looking for something new to make all the viewers at home feel even more that they are at the event itself, rather than sat on their sofas.

My main role is working as a spotter (see Chapter Eight), something which led to Sky doing a feature about me in its magazine where I was described as the 'Carol Vorderman of darts'. It's not a role where you can expect to be given any time to think about all the possibilities. If a player is set up to win a game when he comes to the board, then I have to know, pretty much instantaneously, what combination they're going to use to shoot that score. But it's not that straightforward as, although every player will have a preferred 'out' on any given score, it doesn't always mean that's the one they'll go for. Take 121 for example. The Dutch players, such as Michael van Gerwen and Raymond van Barneveld, will usually look to check out on bullseye, treble 13 and double 16 – or, on another day, they'll go for outer bull (25), treble 20 and double 18. But the British players are more likely, although not absolutely certain, to go for treble 20, 11 and bullseye. But then another player may opt for treble 20, outer bull and double 18.[4]

And that's just one of 162 numbers between two (double one) and 170 (treble 20, treble 20, bullseye) that a darts player can check out on, whether that be with one, two or all three darts. Each of them will have their preferred way of checking out on any number and Sky producers expect me to call it so that the camera will focus on the part of the board where each of their shots is going to land. I'm not in the venue itself though. I'll be in an outside broadcast truck looking at four monitors, although there will be times during a match when I'm focusing on a player and trying to work out what he might be thinking by looking at his body language, or even the way his eyebrows might move as he approaches the board.

I always enjoy my spotting, but the most memorable session of all was when I was working during a match between Phil

---

4 How many of you have just checked to see if those permutations add up to 121?

Taylor and James Wade with Stephen Fry, a big darts fan, also in attendance as a special guest in the studio. I went up to him to say hello and he responded by saying, 'Mr Deller, 138 finish.' He knows a lot about darts, especially during the 1980s.

So he was an easy guest to have and he worked on a game with the main team before coming over to the truck to watch me spotting. As he settled down, Stephen said, 'I have heard about your spotting,' but, when he saw me at work, he was blown away. He could not believe how quickly I gave out the scores needed, especially as I was constantly under pressure to get it right absolutely every time and to do so very quickly.

'Keith, you must have a maths degree?'

I don't, of course, and he was very surprised to hear that. It was all hugely enjoyable and made even more so by the fact that Phil was on top form, hitting two nine-dart finishes in the match. The inhabitants of the truck, I have to tell you, were going mad on what, darts-wise and for me, was a very special night.

Stephen was, and is, of course, a massive star of television, stage and film. That's something I'll never be able to say although I did, at one point, feel like I was becoming so much of a regular on various televisions shows that it might have affected my darts. But at least they all featured darts, in one way or the other, and that suited me as anything that got the sport in front of a mainstream television audience was not only good for my profile (and it all helped in getting good bookings), it was also good for the game as well.

I particularly enjoyed appearing on *Record Breakers* with the late, great Roy Castle. I was attempting to go around the board in doubles but just failed to break that record, although I then had a go at breaking the record for completing three legs of 301. It stood at one minute and 58 seconds but I did it, on the show, in one minute and 47 seconds, which meant I was now the holder of a world record. I also did *Surprise Surprise* with Cilla Black. Eric Bristow and I were sent to a large travellers' camp in Berkshire where I teamed up with Cheryl Baker from the group Bucks Fizz to take on Eric and a big fan of his at the camp. We lost but it was great fun, although a day out somewhere, whatever I ended up doing, was always enjoyable when Eric was involved.

One of the most frequent things I hear about myself is how I broke the darts mould, that old-fashioned image of the game being played by fat blokes who downed their pints of beer almost as quickly as they threw their darts. That didn't mean I wasn't averse to a drink however, and, one year, in recognition of that, I was invited along to the Great British Beer Festival at Olympia where Eric and I were to take it in turns to try and break the record for one leg of 301, which was then 27 seconds. I managed to do it in 25 seconds and there it was, another world record for me.

The roar of the crowd and the smell of the greasepaint summoned me from semi-retirement in 2009 when Channel Four made a programme called *When Boris Met Dave*, which was about Boris Johnson and David Cameron. When David

Cameron was at university, he watched my World Championship win and found it inspiring enough for him to want to make his way to the top – in his case as prime minister rather than becoming world darts champion.

People have always been interested in me – even the sort of folk you wouldn't expect to have any interest in darts. In 1988, the author Martin Amis got in touch and asked if he could interview me and Kim. We readily agreed, and he took us out to lunch where, much to his surprise, I had a soft drink. We met in a wine bar in Enfield and, while I was dressed smartly and content to sip on mineral waters all afternoon if necessary, Martin was smoking his roll-ups and enjoying a beer.

The interview ended up appearing in *The Observer*, which was nice as it meant that darts wasn't just being featured in the red-top papers but was also of interest to the posh ones as well! Martin described me in the interview as 'young and apple-cheeked, a breath of fresh air', adding 'It would have suited my preconceptions if I had found Keith half-drunk in some roadhouse, smothered in tattoos and darts magazines.' The fact that he didn't heightened the appeal and he used his meeting with Kim and I as part of his research for a novel called *London Fields*, in which the main character is an aspiring darts player by the name of Keith Talent. In 2018 the book was made into a film and if, thanks to Martin, Keith Talent is based on me, then I was played by Jim Sturgess. But I'm not complaining about that as Jim is a handsome sort of bloke, although he is quite a bit younger than me.

Looking back at this and all the other chapters in this book, it often strikes me how my life might have been completely different had my parents decided it wasn't worth the bother of putting up that dartboard in the kitchen at home. And I could have understood that; all those tiny little holes in the door, the lino and kitchen units where a dart or three might have gone astray – was it worth it?

Perhaps, with Dad also being into his bowls, I might have taken that sport up instead. But a place was found for that dartboard in the kitchen and, although it would perhaps be an exaggeration to say my life changed from that moment, it certainly played a very big part in how everything went from that day onwards. I have referred to it more than once in the book as it is one of those pivotal moments in time we all have where something that may, at the time, seem inconsequential, is actually hugely significant. So I'll thank them both for doing what they did here. Sadly, Dad passed away in 2013 after a short illness. I'd been away, working on the Grand Slam of Darts for Sky while Dad was in hospital and it was clear, by then, to all of us that he was very poorly indeed.

I eventually asked his doctors how long he had to live and they told me that it was a matter of weeks. I couldn't tell my Mum straight away but, after a few days, we told her that he didn't have long left. Dad lasted for another couple of weeks and then, peacefully and, like the man he was, without any fuss, he slipped away at home as he watched his favourites, *Laurel and Hardy* and *Dad's Army*, on television.

On the day of the funeral the hearse pulled up outside. His coffin was draped with a scarf of his beloved football team Chelsea, as he'd been brought up very close to their ground. I told Mum that the car had arrived and, as we went outside, she saw the coffin and nearly collapsed, so I had to hold her up and help her into the car.

You may well know what this feels like as you'll have gone through times like this yourself with lost loved ones. All I can say is that, recalling those moments right now hurts like you wouldn't believe, but I want this to be in the book.

At the wake, we were talking to friends and family. My children and their friends were absolute stars at darts pairs and were playing, so I wandered over to watch them. Mum was already there so I said to her, 'Come on, you're my partner here. Everyone has three lives, beat the score.' Mum and I won and, believe me, it wasn't for the lack of trying as I have never wanted to win a game of darts so much.

Dad would have been delighted that we were playing darts at his wake.

11

More Stories

*Like I said earlier, you could end up getting
star-struck at these events!*

IF THERE is just one sport that men and women of other
competitive disciplines love to play in their spare time, then it
has to be golf.

Similarly, if there was just one sport that all of those
professionals would probably, given the choice, choose to play at
a competitive level, even at the expense of their own discipline,
then yes, it would probably be golf.

There's something about it that brings out the Dustin
Johnson and Nelly Korda in all of us.

From my perspective, I'd come a long way since being told
to declare to the nation that it was one of my hobbies (when
it wasn't) when I appeared as a guest on *Nationwide* shortly
after my World Championship win. I got so interested in golf
that, by the late 1990s, I was a regular on the celebrity golf

circuit, and, what's more, I did it without being tempted to buy a comfortable pair of slacks or a jumper made by that company from Scotland.

What was particularly enjoyable about the celebrity golf days I went on was the socialising in the evenings. There'd always be a nice sit-down meal at the end of a hard day's work toiling in and out of the rough, plus, when the meal was over, you'd usually be able to sit back and watch some of the more well-known attendees on the day standing up and doing a little routine for everyone. You could end up getting star-struck really and I was guilty of doing so on one particular occasion.

One of my favourite memories is when I met Don Felder. A lot of you may not have even heard of Don but let me tell you, as far as I was concerned, the opportunity to meet him was one that I was not going to turn down. Don is a musician, singer and songwriter and was, from 1974 through to 2001, a member of The Eagles (one of my favourite bands) and is, along with Don Henley and Glenn Frey, one of the co-writers and composers of their most famous song, 'Hotel California'.

So yes, given all that and my love of their music, it's fair to say I was looking forward to the prospect of meeting Don.

I knew the ex-Manchester United footballer Willie Morgan, who was great friends with Don. Willie had, as a result of their friendship, invited him along to one of his golf days. As soon as I knew he was coming, I was on to Willie, asking him if he could arrange for me to meet Don, which he promptly did, and on the day Don came over and said hello.

At the meal after the event, the organiser, a chap by the name of Alan Clarke, introduced all of the celebrities who were there to everyone else. It was the standard sort of thing, who they were, what they did and, if relevant, some of the things they'd achieved which, for me, was useful, as Alan was able to introduce me and mention that I was a former darts world champion. It was nice for me to hear that being said in front of all of those other well-known people and, as I sat at the bar later on that evening, enjoying a beer, I was in a pretty good place.

Which soon got a lot better. Because Don saw me standing there and walked straight over to where I was, saying, 'My man Keith, world champion!' He knew who I was now. We had a beer together and he was, to my surprise, completely taken aback when I told him that The Eagles were my favourite group, 'Hotel California' was my favourite song and that I pretty much knew all the words to the rest of their songs as well.

Like I said earlier, you could end up getting star-struck at these events!

Later on that evening, the musician John Miles, who was Tina Turner's musical director for 13 years, got up and, along with former Lindisfarne keyboard player Brendan Healey, together with Don, started to jam for around 20 minutes or so. Don even played the opening few bars of Hotel California, saying, as he did so, 'This is for my buddy Keith.' I thought I'd died and gone to heaven.

On another trip we were all travelling up on a VIP coach that had copious amounts of champagne and beer stacked up at the back. There were quite a few famous faces on this trip, including Sir Norman Wisdom, the comics Norman Collier and Stan Boardman, the Liverpool manager Roy Evans and the former Everton player and manager Howard Kendall. So quite an eclectic mix. We'd just left Carden Park in Cheshire in order to play at the St Pierre golf course and the drinks were flowing. We had a stop to make on the way, however, to attend Rick Wakeman's son's wedding. I took the opportunity to have a word with Sir Norman, and asked him how he had come up with the words of the song 'Don't Laugh At Me Cause I'm A Fool'. Sir Norman said he was making the film *Trouble in Store* and, during a break from filming, one of the producers had approached him saying, 'We need a song, Norman.' Sir Norman was only too glad to oblige and wrote the track in his break. What a remarkable gift to be able to write such a heartfelt and famous song as that one so quickly and what a talented and very nice man he was. One other little detail about this event is that there was a bar at the wedding. Nothing unusual about that you might think, but think again: this bar was at the back of the altar at the church.

At another event at Carden Park my friend and top darts player Jamie Harvey was at the dinner with me and we were sat next to the famous American singer Johnny Mathis. Jamie can do a pretty good impression of Johnny and, now that he was sat next to the man in question, he wasn't going to let an opportunity like this one get away easily. So he leaned over and said to Johnny, 'I'm a big fan of yours.'

'Thanks mate,' replied Johnny, probably thinking that was the end of it. But no, nothing fazed Jamie, who now launched himself into 'When a Child Is Born'. That was enough for Johnny, who promptly made a sharp exit. I don't know why as it was not only funny but Jamie sounded exactly like Johnny.

It wasn't unusual to have more than a few laughs at Carden Park though. I remember another event which saw the dinner being held on the same day as John and Karen Lowe's wedding anniversary. They were enjoying their evening with a bottle of champagne when our friend Shel Macrae, who once sang with The Fortunes, was doing the cabaret. He'd noticed that John and Karen were there and celebrating their big day together, so he called down to them and said he wanted to sing The Fortunes' biggest hit and dedicate it to the two of them. The song in question is called 'You've Got Your Troubles', which didn't go down too well at the time but, fortunately, John and Karen soon saw the funny side of it.

I sat with another musician at a different event who was persuaded to stand up and give us a song after dinner one evening, so he sang 'Make It With You'. However, I didn't have a clue who the singer was, so as unobtrusively as possible I called Kim on my phone, got her to listen to a bit and then asked her if she had any idea.

It was David Gates, who was the co-lead singer with the band Bread. Kim was, to say the least, green with envy, as the band and that song in particular are one of her favourites, and there I was, completely blasé about it and wondering who he was.

In 2018, I was playing in the British Par 3 Championship at the beautiful Nailcote Hall course near Coventry. We were all set for a good day's golf in an event that was being televised by Sky Sports and, at breakfast, I found myself sat next to the New Zealand golfer Michael Campbell, who had in 2005 won the US Open, one of the game's major tournaments. We were having a chat about darts and golf as Michael waited to start his round, which looked as if it was going to commence in the pouring rain. This was the day when the professional golfers were each paired with a celebrity and I was due to go out a lot later on, as 'my' professional, Steven Tiley, was the current leader (and would go on to win the £50,000 first prize). As it was raining really hard, I felt a little sorry for Michael and, as I had a spare golfing umbrella in my car, I said I'd pop out and get it for him, for which he was very grateful. Off he went, umbrella in hand but, as he and his caddie were walking down the second fairway, his caddie said to him, 'Michael, you're going to have to take the umbrella down.'

'What?' said Michael. 'Don't be stupid, it's still pouring with rain.'

'I know,' replied the caddie. 'But look at what is written on it.'

The symbols and lettering on my spare umbrella spelled out 'Gentleman's Club'. This was from the Circus Tavern, but neither Michael, his caddie nor the viewers on Sky Sports were to know that and they would have been thinking of another kind of 'gentleman's club', one that Michael was now proudly advertising. Michael quickly put the umbrella down and opted to get wet instead.

Later in the day, as I was sat at the bar having a drink along with some of the other celebrity golfers, Michael saw me and came striding over, saying, 'You, Mr Deller!' I was wondering what on earth could have been wrong and he soon told me, giving both me and everyone who was sat nearby a good laugh. To this day, I wish I'd given him my Ipswich Town umbrella instead.

Sometimes I am asked to play the occasional game of darts as part of my television work. Back in 2010, a gentleman got in touch to say he was part of a team putting together a programme for Sky One which would see the TV presenter and actor Justin Lee Collins take up darts from scratch with the intention of taking part in a BDO tournament with the final stages of it played on television. My role was to coach and mentor Justin and to see how far along the competitive path we could get him.

Our first meeting was at my local, The Greyhound in Flempton. Justin came along with his director and a cameraman and we filmed from 6.30pm through to 9.30pm. They were all staying locally at the Bedford Lodge in Newmarket, which was full of horse owners and trainers as the filming had been scheduled at the same time as the Guineas Festival. Once the filming was finished, I suggested to the director and cameraman that they head off back to the Bedford Lodge while I, along with Kim, took Justin to the kebab shop in Mildenhall before dropping him off at the hotel.

I was quite pleased we'd finished filming relatively early as I had to pick up Eric Bristow at 9am the following day from The Bell hotel in Mildenhall, as we were due to be working at the festival the next day. Famous last words. We said we'd have a quick one 'for the road' before, eventually, leaving the pub for the kebab shop at 1.45am, late enough for me to call the shop and ask them to stay open a little bit longer than they would normally as I had a famous person with me and he'd be more than happy to let them take a few photos of him there, which Justin did.

So Justin ended up being dropped off at the hotel at about 2.15am, while I got to bed three-quarters of an hour later. I still had to pick Eric up in just a few hours, which I did, and we opened at Newmarket, as scheduled, at 9.30am. Justin turned up at noon, looking as white as the proverbial sheet, and could not believe we'd both been at the racecourse since much earlier that same morning. He then gave Eric a game, Eric kicking it off by telling Justin he'd rip his head off which, of course, is exactly what he proceeded to do, winning easily. Then, a month later, I went down to Bristol along with my son Matt who gave Justin another good beating, scoring 140 to defeat him in front of the TV cameras which, for a 15-year-old, was very good going – but exactly what Justin didn't want as far as his confidence was concerned. It showed. Justin lost 3-0 in the first round of the BDO competition, but overall the training had gone well and the final programme was, I think, very entertaining and certainly worth watching.

Kim and I aren't celebrity groupies but we do tend to find ourselves at places and events where there might be a fair few of them scattered about the place, and none more so than when we find ourselves in one of our favourite places in the world, Las Vegas. I was playing in a tournament out there once when Engelbert Humperdinck invited some of the top players there to watch his show as well as have a few games of darts afterwards. I would have loved to have gone along but Kim and I had a prior engagement, tickets to go and see Siegfried and Roy, the entertainers and magicians who were famous for performing with white tigers and lions as part of their act. It was a good show but I couldn't help thinking about what might have been happening with Engelbert and the lads and later found out that they had graciously given him a 100 start in the games, but it had backfired on them somewhat as he kept beating them.

Some years before that, I was taking part in a darts tournament at the Sahara Hotel in Vegas at the same time as the group Kool & the Gang were playing there. I was enjoying my breakfast one morning and was passing the time of day with a friendly American who was sat next to me.

'I'm over here playing darts,' I said, adding, 'Are you on holiday?'

He looked me straight in the eye and answered, 'I am the lead singer of Kool & the Gang.'

Oops.

At that precise moment, let me tell you, I did not feel at all cool in the presence of Robert 'Kool' Bell.

In 2018 I was on holiday in Vegas rather than working. It just so happened that, while I was out there, the World Series of Darts was being played. Robbie Williams was also out there playing a few concerts at the Wynn Hotel and it just happens that I've known Pete Conway, Robbie's dad, for quite a few years. I met up with Pete and told him that I was in town with Kim, along with her brother John and his wife Sally. Pete duly invited us all to watch one of Robbie's shows as well as popping backstage afterwards to meet him. We did so, as did darts player Peter Wright and his wife Jo. Robbie saw us and came over to say hello, asking me if I was still playing. He went on to say that he remembered that when he was young, Pete had taken him along to see me play in an exhibition in Stoke-on-Trent – that had been a while ago. He was, you won't be surprised to learn, brilliant throughout his show that night, starting with him descending down on to the stage by means of assorted wires and a harness. Just as he had made his entry there was a small earthquake in the area, which caused a bit of disturbance and had a worried Robbie thinking that there was something wrong with his gear and wondering what might be about to happen.

12

Darting Ahead

The reception I got this time was a
little more hostile, to say the least ...

BY 2019 I was pretty set in my working ways and routine, which
suited me with a mix of doing my exhibitions and working for
Sky.

That year's PDC World Championship was notable in that
it saw an increase in the number of competitors from 72 to 96,
a far cry from when I'd won the BDO title in 1983, when there
had been a total entry of 32, including the qualifiers, with a total
prize fund available of £33,050. Now, nearly four decades later,
an additional 64 players would be fighting it out for a total prize
amount of £2.5m, with the winner getting £500,000.

My cheque for winning the BDO title had been £8,000.
The times, as someone once sang, were a changin'.

Thinking about that, I'm often asked if I wish the same
sort of money had been available to win in my day, or if I am

jealous of the huge amounts of money available to today's leading players. It's an all too easy question to ask and it applies to most sports, especially football, where some of the salaries in today's Premier League might be 500 times, or even more, the amount some of the Ipswich Town players were getting back in the 1980s. But no, I'm not jealous, not at all. When I won the World Championship in 1983, the average weekly wage was £60 a week and, within three months of winning that title, I'd bought a house in Enfield that had a swimming pool. I was 23 years old at the time. How many people of my age back then were able to buy properties like that or earn £400 a night doing exhibition work? I'm not jealous because the times back then were great for me just as they were for Eric Bristow, John Lowe, Jocky Wilson and all the other leading players of the day.

That's all very well and good Keith, people will say. But you won £8,000 while Gerwyn Price, who won the 2021 PDC World Championship, took home half a million quid, while the players who went out in the first round got £7,500 for their troubles. How is that fair?

I understand where their argument is coming from. But look at it another way. Leighton Rees got £3,000 for winning the very first BDO World Championship in 1978. It only took five years for my take-home for winning to not be far off triple that. It's about progress and how the game has developed over the last four and a bit decades. And it's the same for every sport. I looked up how much Virginia Wade, the last British woman to win the ladies' singles at Wimbledon, received in prize money when she won the title in 1977: £13,500. Now, fast forward to the last British man to win the gents' singles at the same tournament, Andy Murray in 2016, who took £2m, an increase of £120,000 from the previous year. Is that unfair? No, it's how tennis, its development, coverage and big money sponsorship has grown over the intervening years, just as darts has.

Today's best players deserve the big money because darts is now one of the most watched, and participated in, sports in the world. Commercially, the tournaments are a huge success. They always sell out within hours of the tickets going on sale and the audiences present in some of the arenas we play in today are bigger than those at most League One and some Championship football matches.

This huge commercial growth also helps the players from my generation. The likes of Bobby George and myself, for example, benefit hugely from the big money that is available at exhibitions, which are as popular with the audiences today as the big tournaments are. That money is also an acknowledgement to today's top players for the work they put in away from the cameras and public eye, with countless hours every single day spent practising on their own before being expected, on cue, to perform for the millions watching them on demand.

So did Gerwyn deserve his £500,000? Of course he did.

Now that I've answered that question, let's return to the subject in hand, the 2019 PDC World Championship. The field was made up of the top 32 from the PDC's Order of Merit, the 32 highest-ranked players on the PDC Pro Tour and 32 qualifiers from around the world, including two female players, England's Lisa Ashton and Anastasia Dobromyslova from Russia. Also among the qualifiers were players from Brazil, Hong Kong, Lithuania, Singapore, South Africa and the Philippines. Back in 1983, over half of the entrants had been British.

Darts had become well and truly a global game being played to a massive worldwide audience. But, more than that, the leading players were fast becoming sporting superstars in their own right. Phil Taylor was definitely one of the true superstars, but he'd retired the previous year after losing in the 2018 final to Rob Cross, 30 years his junior. Phil spoke after that match, telling the BBC, 'I tried my best but he was like me 25 years ago, he was relentless and didn't stop putting me under pressure … he's dedicated, he's listened, learned and the players next year have got a big problem … it was like an old man against a young man, it was a mis-match. That's it for me because I haven't got the energy or interest to beat Michael van Gerwen or him.'

The times really were a changin'.

Michael van Gerwen won the 2019 title, beating Michael Smith in the final. MVG is, believe me, an unbelievable talent. Another question I'm always being asked is who is the greatest player, Michael or Phil Taylor? Here's my answer to that one as well.

I'll start by talking about Michael. He won the World Masters in 2006 when he was 17 years old, an unbelievable achievement for someone so young. But then he had been playing darts at a seriously competitive level for four years by then already, so that was his reward for all the hard work he'd put in. Phil was, at around that time, at his peak. He'd won 11 out of 12 world titles from 1995 to 2006 before winning it again in 2009, 2010 and 2013. Then Michael really started to make his presence felt, winning the World Championship in 2014, 2017 and 2019 as well as the World Matchplay in 2015 and 2016 and the Grand Slam of Darts over three consecutive years from 2015 to 2017.

Phil then retired in 2018, citing Michael as one of the players he believed he no longer had the 'energy' to beat anymore. So was that a case of the King of Darts is dead, long live the King?

Well, no. Not quite. Michael was on the sort of winning run that we'd only ever seen before with Phil, and the three-dart averages he was hitting, such as 102.21 in the 2019 world final, were so good and the standard he was playing at was so high that we were beginning to think yes, just as Phil had done before him, the man from the Netherlands was looking as if he was going to dominate the game for years. But it never quite happened because, unlike with Phil, who had no real close contenders for his crown, Michael found that some of the newer players coming through, such as Peter Wright and Gerwyn Price, winners of the last two PDC World Championships in 2020 and 2021 respectively, were more than capable of taking the big titles themselves. Peter beat Michael in the 2020 final and, although Michael averaged 102.88, Peter basically matched him with 102.79. He also scored over 100 62 times in that match, hit 11 180s and had one checkout on 140; fantastic darts all the way in what was an enthralling final.

So, in conclusion, as wonderful a player as Michael is, he hasn't been able to dominate in the way that Phil did and with, at the time of writing, Gerwyn and Peter first and second respectively in the PDC Order of Merit, he has a lot of work to do, as they all do, to be an undisputed number one over the sort of time period that Phil was.

Phil Taylor is, and will always be for me, the greatest darts player of all time. Will someone come along and be even better than him though? Time will tell and I am looking forward to seeing who the up and coming challengers will be in the years ahead.

* * *

I was back on spotting duties with Sky 12 months later for the 2020 World Championship, which maybe saw a slight surprise at its conclusion when Peter won it, beating Michael in that final. Peter had been seeded seventh so was expected to make his exit at the quarter-final stage, but he blew everyone away and was a deserved winner. Sky did another tremendous job with the coverage, going as far as to set up a special channel, Sky Sports Darts, and involving lots of players with its commentary team, including Wayne Mardle and Rod Harrington as well as Laura Turner from the BDO. It was hard work (don't let anyone ever tell you it is a 'jolly'; take it from me, it most definitely isn't) but hugely enjoyable once again.

Shortly after I'd completed my spotting duties at Alexandra Palace, Kim and I headed out to Australia to visit her brothers before the whole family set off for a cruise in and around Australia and New Zealand. As we were on an ocean liner, I didn't have to tuck my sheets in every night to keep the spiders out, which was a bonus. We all had a thoroughly enjoyable time, so much so that we knew, come the end of the holiday, it would be really hard to say goodbye and head our separate ways again, so we decided to stop off in Singapore for five days, the part of our holiday I won't ever forget as it was while we were there that we heard the first reports from China about this strange and hitherto unknown virus that had seemingly originated in a place called Wuhan.

The reports and information we heard were worrying, more so because Singapore is only five hours by air away from China, and there were plenty of flights happening between the two countries. But, even so, we'd be heading home soon and we all consoled ourselves by thinking that, as serious as the virus might turn out to be, it would never reach the UK. We wouldn't have been the only ones to think that way as the weeks and months sped by.

Once we'd returned home, I got to work on the Premier League nights for Sky, expecting, for the most part, the rest of the year and for life to carry on pretty much as usual. I'd also started doing some shows and enjoyed one great night in particular at Trinity Park in Ipswich with Wayne Mardle, Colin Lloyd and Bobby George. I'd also started doing darts nights at a club called Infernos in London, which were also a lot of fun, as well as, I hope, bringing darts and the all-round entertainment it can be to a whole new demographic. Sky Sports then televised the Premier League double-header over in Rotterdam. We thought, at the time, it would end up being one of the last big events that Raymond van Barneveld competed in, so what was always going to be a lively occasion was even more so with 11,000 Dutch fans making up an ocean of boisterous orange on both nights. Unforgettable stuff.

If that was a raucous event, then one that followed up soon afterwards was anything but. Kim and I had been invited to The Dorchester in London for a black-tie night. It was very smart and certainly no sea of orange shirts to be seen there. Two of the people sat at our table were particularly interesting company; one was the man who designed Tottenham Hotspur's new football stadium, while another was from the professional services company which, among other things, is a business partner and advisor to Manchester United. So there was lots of football talk to be had there and good company all round.

Looking back now, I'm sure that, with the pandemic in mind, a lot of people see 2019 as some sort of golden era, the last year that we all enjoyed when we were able to live, work and socialise under what may end up being called 'the old normal'. Another great event I was privileged to have been invited to was the British Par 3 Championship at the Nailcote Hall golf club in Berkswell. There were some very famous golfing names there with us, including Tony Jacklin, Paul Lawrie and Ian Woosnam, who was the US Masters champion back in 1991. Lots of quality there, especially as the other two are also major tournament winners.

* * *

As far as exhibitions are concerned, I'm looking forward to doing some more work with Lord Russell Baker in the coming years. Lord Baker of Little Moulton devotes much of his life to community funding throughout Norfolk and has, in recent years, put on some memorable events to raise money that have involved some of the biggest names in snooker, including Ronnie O'Sullivan and Steve Davis. Through his business, he now arranges events that also include famous names from the world of football as well as darts. I'm always happy to take part, as are some of my friends and fellow competitors, including John Lowe, while Eric Bristow also appeared at plenty. I knew then that Lord Russell was serious about what he was doing when he first called me up to ask if I'd be interested and when we first met I thought the smartly dressed and very well spoken gent I was with would be more suitable for doing an advert for gin and tonic, rather than immersing himself into the world of darts. But he is good at what he does and I was soon involved in my first occasion with him, a legends tournament in Norwich, which featured me, John, Eric and Bobby George.

The event was held at Carrow Road, the home of Norwich City, Ipswich Town's biggest rivals. There isn't exactly any love lost between the fans of the two clubs and, as a well-known supporter of Ipswich, I got a lukewarm reception at best from the noisy and enthusiastic spectators who packed the place out. They probably ended up liking me even less when I went on to win it, beating John in the final, but it was a good night out and for an excellent cause, so I was more than happy to run the gauntlet in Norfolk again when Lord Russell asked me along to another event he was organising in Norwich. The reception I got this time was a little more hostile to say the least, but I'd half expected that and, for all the stick I might get for being an Ipswich supporter at events that are held primarily in Canary country, I'm looking forward to doing some more shows with Russell, who is a good friend, in the future.

I really enjoy meeting other people who have competed at the very highest levels of sport. The sports that we all play might be very different, but there are always shared experiences we can draw upon – expectation, pressure and dealing with the demands of fame are just three of them, so I like 'comparing notes', so to speak, if I ever get the chance. Mind you, at Nailcote Hall I ended up chatting all night about football to Peter Schmeichel, so much so that, by the time we both decided we'd better get some sleep prior to our game of golf the next day, it was daylight and breakfast time.

You never really know or appreciate how good life can be until aspects of it are taken away from you. Talk of the pandemic, that health issue that we'd first heard about in Singapore but had assumed would only ever be a local issue became more and more widespread, so much so that every news bulletin was soon including a story about Covid-19 and how it was going to affect all of our lives.

It really hit home to us how serious the situation was when we lost a dear friend to the virus. That made cancelling events, holidays and even the introduction of lockdown seem almost inconsequential. Sure, I couldn't go out and play darts. But people were dying, people we knew.

It was getting a little bit frightening. I don't think that Kim and I were the only people who thought, hoped, prayed almost that the pandemic would last for no more than a year and that, by Christmas 2020 our lives would be getting back to normal, especially when, in July 2020, the prime minister stated that he was working on a plan that would see a 'more significant return to normality' by the festive period. That didn't happen, and as the new year beckoned another 'victim' of the pandemic was this book because, as much as we both wanted to, my co-writer Edward Couzens-Lake and I weren't able to get together to work on it.

We adapted, of course. The fact that you are currently reading it is all the proof you'll ever need of that. As so many thousands and thousands of people did, despite the most difficult of circumstances. I was, however, very lucky in that all the darts events due to be covered by television went ahead, albeit in very different circumstances to what we all would have been used to or preferred. This included the 2021 PDC World Championship, which was held at Alexandra Palace from 15 December 2020 to 3 January 2021, with 96 competitors taking part, drawn from 29 different countries, and the whole event was televised to 25 countries all over the world, including Austria, Brazil, Estonia, Iceland and the United States.

Luckily for all of us, the Covid-19 restrictions that were in place at the time meant that the event could go ahead, with Alexandra Palace permitted to have 1,000 fans present, although they were not permitted to wear fancy dress while football-style chanting, a regular feature from the spectators at darts, was also prohibited. Still, we all felt that we'd have been able to put on a good show for what was, essentially, very much a captive audience at home. Ultimately however, we weren't able to do that and, as London entered a new phase of restrictions on 16 December, the entire event, bar the opening night, ended up being held behind closed doors.

It's not the same, of course. How can it be? The atmosphere created at a big darts event is as good, sporting occasion-wise, as that of any other comparable event. It is loud, vibrant and, for the main part, very good-humoured. People are even allowed to have a beer or three at their seats, which you won't be able to do at a football match any time soon in this country. Things didn't run perfectly for, no matter what precautions we all took to prevent Covid affecting it, one player, Martin Kleermaker, had to withdraw after he tested positive for the virus on 20 December while the man who was expected to step up into his place, England's Josh Payne, also had to withdraw after he came into close contact with someone who'd had a positive test.

The tournament could, I guess, have ended up being postponed. But, despite all the difficulties, it was played out to the end with Gerwyn Price winning his first World Championship after beating Gary Anderson in the final and becoming, in the process, the new world number one.

Like everyone else in the game, I drove away from the Ally Pally hoping that the 2022 contest, when it arrives, will see the return of the fans, the noise, the passion and the beer, singing and occasional dancing. It's a joyful event, all darts tournaments are. Yes, the players are looking to win and they'll have put all the hours in beforehand to play and compete as well as possible. But we know that we are, to the fans, entertainers as well as sportsmen and women, and that realisation is, I think, one of the reasons darts translates so well to television and why its popularity continues to grow.

Because, whether you are one of the players or one of the thousands of fans, it's all about having fun and putting a smile on people's faces. And we can all do with some of that after the last 18 months or so. Hopefully I'll be one of the people given the opportunity to do just that.

* * *

What about the future of the game though, especially as we all work our way, slowly, out of a world that has been put on hold in so many ways because of Covid-19?

Who are the players to look out for, the next generation of darts stars?

I like Luke Humphries very much. He has it within himself to go all the way in the game, is dedicated and is making it all the way to finals. Dirk van Duijvenbode is another great talent who has already, as I write this, made a major televised final, so he is not that far away from winning his first big title.

Dimitri Van den Bergh is another player who I can see winning majors over the next few years. Dimitri won the World Matchplay in 2020 and he already has the full darts package. He also looks after himself well and is a very polite young man who, for his sponsors, portrays a fantastic image for our sport.

Then there is, of course, the PDC which, under Barry Hearn and, into the future, Eddie Hearn works so well for the game, guided by its CEO Matt Porter. They have all been very instrumental in what is happening in darts and how the game is continuing to grow, and with them at the helm I can only see even bigger tournaments being arranged with ever growing prize funds attached to them.

The future of our sport is, I firmly believe, in a very good place indeed. But in among all of that, what about Keith Deller?

I still see myself as, first and foremost, a professional darts player. And I still want to compete, which is why the advent of a World Seniors Championship in 2022 has excited me so much.

It all came about when the managers of Michael van Gerwen and snooker player Ronnie O'Sullivan called me to say that the event was on and they were working on getting it shown on television not that, I suspect, Sky for one will need a lot of persuading. They were calls that, if they didn't quite change my life, certainly got my competitive juices flowing again, which I hadn't ever expected to be happening. I was enjoying my work at the exhibitions as well as watching others deal with the pressure of competitive darts through my work on Sky. I'd last entered the PDC World Championship in 2005, while the last major tournament I played in was the UK Open in 2007, when I was knocked out in the second round. That was pretty much it for me and I didn't want to be someone who turned up at all the events just to get knocked out early on, or, worse than that, have to qualify for them against someone who was less than half my age.

No, I was enjoying the career I had outside of the competitive game. And, for nearly 15 years, that was how it was. But not now.

This is different; this is a new challenge. And I'm going to make sure I am ready for it. Martin Adams, John Lowe and Phil Taylor are just three of the names taking part, so there are going to be some former world champions out there, and they'll be as hungry as I am for getting up on that stage in front of the television cameras and firmly in the spotlight once again. We aren't in the first flush of youth anymore, or, in the case of some, even the second. But we can all still play darts and we'll not only want to prove that to the people we're up against, we'll want to do it for ourselves as well.

I've started already. I've done my garage out, complete with a big TV and carpet. It looks good and, more to the point, when I'm in there, as I am a lot right now, it feels good as well. It feels as if I am back in the game, looking the part and wanting to win.

So things were starting to happen, and then Loxley Darts got in touch wanting to sign me up, which excited me as much as those initial telephone calls had, because I feel like a world champion again and that can only be a good thing. I've got some new darts coming out but, more than that, the team at Loxley suggested making the colours of my shirt the same as they were when I won the World Championship back in 1983. The shirt and the red trousers. A gimmick? No. I see it as part of getting back into that competitive mindset again, that champion mindset. Thinking like a winner and looking like a winner.

I've also secured another new sponsorship deal with a company called Complete Aluminium Systems, based in Hampshire, another step towards building myself up as a genuine competitor once again who is able to win the big competitions.

It's all about those marginal gains.

I'm now in the golden years of my career. I still love travelling the world and remain very fortunate in that I can go to beautiful places to enjoy the fruits of my work and the success I have had.

So if this is the part of the book where you'd be expecting 61-year-old Keith Deller to be talking about how, after a long career in darts, he's winding things down a bit, taking it easy and spending his time in the local garden centre or planning days out with his wife, you'd be mistaken.

Because the kid from Suffolk is back. He's both feeling and looking the part again. And he wants to win.

Acknowledgements

I WOULD like to thank the people who have helped me throughout my career as well as with the writing of this book.

My wife Kim and children Lauren and Matthew.

Lauren, I have to say, loves her sports and has played for some good ladies' football teams. She also takes after her dad where darts is concerned, winning her ladies' league singles title four years running. I remember playing at an exhibition at Wolverhampton races with Eric Bristow once and saying to her, 'Show Eric how good you are at darts.'

She hit three consecutive bullseyes, which made Eric's jaw drop. I'll never forget the look of surprise on his face when she did that!

I also want to thank:

My late father Derek and my mum, Pamela Deller.

My late father-in-law Alec Ovens and mother-in-law, the late Sheila Ovens.

Winmau darts, Unicorn darts, Darts GB and my new darts manufacturers, Loxley darts.

To my many friends around the UK who have always supported me, including Rab Bain – thank you for 30 years of friendship mate, as well as the sponsorship you have helped to secure for me.

To Sky Sports – 27 years and counting!

To Pitch Publishing and my co-author, Edward Couzens-Lake.

Plus, finally, the two people who took the time out to write such kind words about me for this book, Stephen Fry and Phil Taylor.

Keith Deller

* * *

AS ALWAYS, the names of all the people who have supported me in this, as they do all of my projects, makes up a very long list indeed. But I know who you are and will be seeking you all out to say a personal thank you.

Huge thanks to Paul and Jane Camillin and all at the wonderful Pitch Publishing for believing in yet another one of my proposals. Hugely appreciated.

To Duncan Olner for his creative genius.

Steve Daszko for access to his wonderful photographic archive.

Lord Russell Baker for helping to kick off this project in the first place.

To Spencer Clay for his lovely recollection about playing darts with Keith.

I don't have a sponsor so if you'd like to be thanked in my next book, please get in touch!

I must also mention my own late father, Gordon Lake. While Keith was working his way towards World Championship glory in 1983, I was in the run up to taking my A-level exams that spring, which meant plenty of revision and early nights, all coinciding with my return to college at the latter stages of the tournament. As it progressed I would, every morning, stumble my way downstairs (not) ready for another day where I would be greeted by my dad, who would, over his breakfast, inform me that, 'the boy Deller won again'.

Those daily updates were my first introduction to the world of darts, a game Dad played and enjoyed and, of course, to Keith Deller who, even though he was an Ipswich fan, was still a fellow man of East Anglia, so I dutifully followed his career from that time onwards. Dad would, I suspect, be rather proud of me for ending up co-writing 'the boy Deller's' book.

To Kim Deller for her insights into life with Keith at home and on the stage.

And, finally, to Keith himself for all of his hard work, dedication and diligence from day one. It takes two people to put together a book like this one and it has felt as if we have worked as a team throughout. A true professional and a gentleman as well.

Edward Couzens-Lake
August 2021

Also available at all good book stores

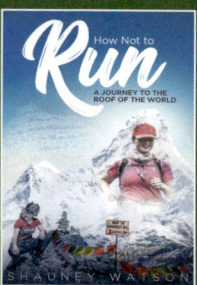

9781785314537

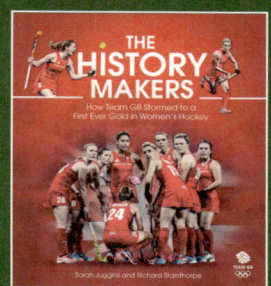

9781785313301

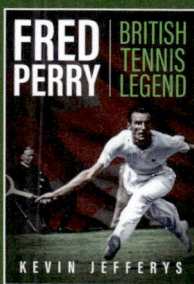

9781785312908

9781785314452

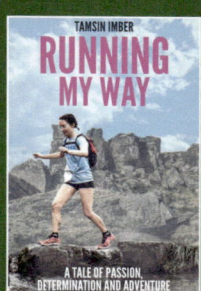

9781785314544

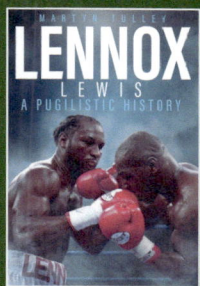

9781785313295

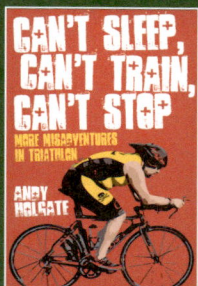

9781909178335

9781785314513

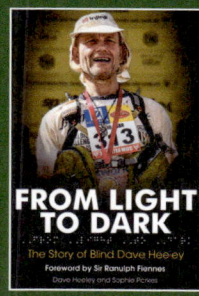

9781785312298